PURPOSE DRIVEN WOMAN

PURPOSE DRIVEN WOMAN

◆

The Time Is Now

to walk in the full manifestation of who God created YOU to be!

DANIELLA AKOSUA

Purpose Driven Woman

Copyright © 2019 by Daniella Akosua

All rights reserved. This book or any portion thereof may not be reproduced or used in any manner whatsoever without the express written permission of the publisher except for the use of brief quotations in a book review.

Scripture taken from the Holy Bible, NEW INTERNATIONAL VERSION®, NIV® Copyright © 1973, 1978, 1984, 2011 by Biblica, Inc.® Used by permission. All rights reserved worldwide. Scripture taken from the New King James Version. Copyright © 1982 by Thomas Nelson, Inc. Used by permission. All rights reserved. Scripture quotations taken from the Amplified® Bible (AMP), Copyright © 2015 by The Lockman Foundation. Used by permission. www.Lockman.org.

Printed in the United Kingdom
First Printing, 2019

ISBN: 9781070423616 (Paperback)
Imprint: Independently published

Acknowledgements

Firstly, I would like to give thanks and glory to the Almighty God, My Abba, for directing me to write this book and for giving me the courage and boldness to *actually* put the words He inspired on paper, in order to release it to this generation. It definitely has not been by my own might or strength, but simply by the Spirit of God. Therefore, I am very grateful to Him.

To everyone who has been with me on this journey, you know who you are, all your encouragement, words of wisdom and support has been very influential in pushing me to become the woman I am today. I love and appreciate you all.

Dedication

Dear reader, I now dedicate this book to you. Through every chapter, every paragraph, every sentence and every word, God had you in mind. Therefore, Woman of Purpose, I pray that you allow these words to be sown deeply into your heart and spirit in order for you to live and function as the woman God predestined you to be: a Purpose Driven Woman.

Table of Contents

1. Purpose: Existed Before Existence...1

2. "I Don't Know MY Purpose!" …………………….........19
   - *Do Not Live Somebody Else's Purpose*

3. Laying The Right Foundation…………………………..31
   - *Identity Breeds Purpose*
   - *Self-Love*
   - *Emotional Healing*

4. God Says "Walk With Me…" ………………….....……..75
   - *The Sheep of His Pasture*
   - *"Walk with Me as Moses Walked with Me"*
   - *Seek God, Not The Assignment*

5. Embrace Every Season, Enjoy The Journey……………...105
   - *Understand Your Own Times and Seasons*

6. Set Boundaries, Have Standards…………………....…119

7. Step Out & Step Up…………………………….....…...137
   - *Salt & Light*
   - *The Daughters of Zelophehad*

8. The Time Is NOW……………………………..….……157

You are a Purpose Driven Woman……………….........166
Author Bio…………………………………………….........167

1

Purpose:

Existed Before Existence

Psalm 139:13-16 NIV

13 For you created my inmost being;

you knit me together in my mother's womb.

14 I praise you because I am fearfully and wonderfully made,

your works are wonderful,

I know that full well.

15 My frame was not hidden from you

when I was made in the secret place,

when I was woven together in the depths of the earth.

16 Your eyes saw my unformed body;

all the days ordained for me were written in your book

before one of them came to be.

PURPOSE: EXISTED BEFORE EXISTENCE

If anyone is to ask me what scripture best describes purpose, I would say the one above; especially verse 16. This passage of scripture simply makes you understand that you existed before you even came into existence. Honestly, how amazing is that!

> *~ Purpose = the life God planned for you to live and the assignments He assigned to you to fulfil before you were born. ~*

The first time I ever came across this scripture, verse 16 in particular, my mind was literally blown away. I was in my bedroom at university and my whole perspective of life changed. I mean I knew that God knew my end from beginning, I knew "before I was formed in my mother's womb, He knew me", I knew all of that good stuff we hear all the time. But when God plainly speaks to you *personally* through His written word, it is different, everything changes. You gain a personal understanding and revelation for yourself. It becomes REAL to YOU.

Sometimes, you can hear or read something time and time again, but the significance of what is being read or said doesn't really dawn on you. However, there comes a time when a different light shines on those words, and you are able to grasp a deeper understanding. That was my experience exactly. I remember saying: *"Oh my goodness, what if that which I am doing right now on this very day is not what has been written; what if it's not what I am meant to be doing; what if I've gone totally off track?!"*. I was saying the most.

Even though I may have over exaggerated just a little teeny weeny bit, what I also remember saying to myself is *"I actually need to make sure I live the life God planned for me; the life which was written in His books before I even became a clot of blood in my mother's womb. I need to do all I can to live a purposeful life! I can't get this wrong! There are certain things I have been assigned to do, and that is what I will be judged upon at the end of the day."*

It may sound as though coming to this realisation stirred up fear within me, but it wasn't fear, it was simply a desire and a determination to do all I could and all I needed to do in order to live a meaningful and purposeful life, and hear "well done my good and faithful servant" on that day. We must all come to this point of realising that we were born on purpose, not by accident; and because we were born on purpose, we must live on purpose, and not live by accident. You cannot live anyhow. You must be able to come to the realisation that YOU have a responsibility to fulfil all the words that were written about you in God's books before creation.

PURPOSE: EXISTED BEFORE EXISTENCE

The day God brought you into this earth was not a coincidence. When God decided to bring you into existence on that day, He had in mind what He needed you to do.

For my 21st birthday, God taught me a big lesson. I wanted to do my 21st big. I mean, it was my 21st. I couldn't just go somewhere, eat and return home; it had to be memorable. However, the day before my 21st birthday, I was in prayer and God spoke; He made me understand that when it comes to my birthday, the most important thing I should be reflecting on is what I have accomplished in the past year that can testify of my purpose gradually being fulfilled. I said, "wow, God that's actually true". It was a revelation which really ministered to me. Hypocritically, my actions thereon-after did not reflect that. I was still so concerned about myself; how I wanted to celebrate, what I needed to wear, what wig I needed to purchase, the dress I would wear on my "birthday Sunday".

I wasn't getting the picture so God really put me in check. Everything I was organising was not going according to plan. The weekend I initially wanted to celebrate on, I wasn't able to because a church programme was scheduled to take place that weekend. The alternative weekend I had chosen was also unavailable because another youth programme had been scheduled. I got frustrated. "But it's my

21st, it's not fair that I have to cancel my plans because of church programmes". I sounded so carnal, haha. As a result, I *did* celebrate but not in the grand style I wanted.

The day of your birthday should be a reminder to you that you are here to fulfil your purpose. I'm not trying to say celebrating your birthday isn't necessary, but the truth of the matter is that it is secondary. Every year when it comes to the day of your birth, the **main** question you must be asking yourself is: how closer am I getting to completing the assignments assigned to my life in order to fulfil divine purpose. Not where the best restaurant to eat is.

To be Purpose Driven, you need to be driven by purpose; whereby everything you do in life is motivated by your desire to fulfil every word spoken concerning you. Fulfilling purpose must be the driving force behind everything you do. Otherwise, you fall into the danger of living a life that may seem meaningful to you but may not necessarily be meaningful in the eyes of God.

Let's look at two people from the bible whom we can evidently see were ordained even before their existence.

We'll look at Moses first. You may be thinking why we are looking at men as examples and not women even though the book is targeted for women. This book will focus on both men and women. The reason being: "We are entering into a dispensation whereby God is raising more women who will begin to operate "like men". Women of this generation will begin to carry such an anointing which will surpass that of men who refuse or fail to fulfil the purpose of their existence. This will then usher women even more into apostolic ministries." This is a prophetic statement, which was declared by one of my brothers, Henry Agyeman. Receive it in Jesus Name. Women, it is time to arise!

Moses is one of my favourite people in the bible because he truly is someone whom I relate to on a different level. I believe if God was to liken me to anyone in the bible, it would be him. *"So I have another Moses case here I see, no problem, I know how to handle this; no mind too hard for Me to transform"* is what He would be saying to Himself, but we thank God for His mercy that never gives up on us daily, haha.

Looking at the birth of Moses, and the environment he was also born into, he was basically born into a war zone. From the book of Exodus chapter 1, we see that at the time when the Israelites had become slaves and captives in the land of Egypt, it was at that same time where God decided to bring Moses onto the scene. Though the children of Israel had been enslaved for several years before Moses was born, it is important to realise and understand that _God is Purposeful._

He knew when it was the best time to bring Moses onto the scene, and as a result caused Moses to be born into that generation for a specific purpose: to deliver His people out of the land of Egypt and lead them into the land of Canaan, the promised land. In the same way Moses was born into that generation for a purpose is the same way you also have been born into this generation for a specific purpose. Yes, you. To do something. Every generation faces particular issues or problems that need to be dealt with. For instance, some of the issues that have been very prevalent in past and present generations include issues such as suicide, violent crime, drug abuse, deadly diseases, immoral laws being passed, racism, dysfunctional families, sexual sin, identity confusion, and many more.

Nothing we are seeing in our generation and society today is new; it is not only now that these issues have surfaced. The bible makes us understand there is nothing new under the sun (Ecclesiastes 1:9). Everything happening now has happened before. The only difference is that our adversary, the devil, is becoming more tactical and desperate, and is playing on the ignorance and naivety of believers. He attempts to make us blind to these issues, where we end up believing they are 'normal' and that nothing can be done because they have been ongoing for so long. He tries to make us believe there are certain domains we cannot enter and certain things we do not have the competence to do because we are believers; even though we have been called to dominate all spheres.

However, because of these various different issues that are becoming very much unbearable and detrimental, God will ultimately raise people to deal with and tackle those particular issues.

YOU ARE ONE OF THOSE PEOPLE.

Today's generation of believers must believe and understand they are different and have been called to fix a broken generation and society, in every capacity. We must believe we CAN influence the culture that surrounds us and ALLOW God to raise and develop us as people of purpose. We cannot continue to give the devil license to play on our ignorance. If he is going hard to magnify these issues, we must go harder to solve them.

One thing to also realise is this: the devil knows you have a heavy purpose and mandate upon your life; and because he knows this, he trembles. He will try everything in his *limited* power to distort, disrupt and interfere with the plan and purpose of God for your life. He will try but he will not succeed. We see how he tried with the life of Moses by causing Pharaoh to make such a horrible decree. This decree instructed all the Hebrew midwives to kill every male child that was born from a Hebrew woman (Exodus 1:15-16). Why not the Egyptian women also? *raised eyebrows*

When the devil makes plans, he is specific! He knew Moses had been ordained before his existence, and so targeted the Hebrew women. He knew the impact and influence Moses would have on the nation of Israel in delivering them out of bondage. It is very much the same as the decree King Herod made when he found out our Saviour Jesus Christ would be a threat to his kingship (Matthew 2:1-16). But when God has ordained you before you were even formed in your mother's womb, nothing and nobody can stop it!!

~ People only seek to hinder your purpose and destroy your destiny when they see you as a threat ~

With purpose comes opposition. Pharaoh only decided to make the Israelites slaves and kill every new-born Hebrew male simply because he feared the influence the Israelites had the *potential* to have. He saw them as a threat.

PURPOSE: EXISTED BEFORE EXISTENCE

Exodus 1:9-13 NIV

⁹ *"Look," he said to his people, "the Israelites have become far too numerous for us.*

¹⁰ *Come, we must deal shrewdly with them or they will become even more numerous and, if war breaks out, will join our enemies, fight against us and leave the country."*

¹¹ *So they put slave masters over them to oppress them with forced labor, and they built Pithom and Rameses as store cities for Pharaoh.*

¹² *But the more they were oppressed, the more they multiplied and spread; so the Egyptians came to dread the Israelites*

¹³ *and worked them ruthlessly.*

Moses was a threat before he was even born, and because he was a threat, his life was targeted before the very day he was born. The devil targeted his life and tried to eliminate him and remove him from the scene as soon as he entered the scene, but we thank God for people with vision and discernment: his mother. The spiritual attacks I encountered just two days after I started to write this book have amused me. The devil was trembling because he knew this book would end up in your hands on this very day, and would be influential in your pursuit to understanding the importance of purpose, as well as becoming a purpose driven woman.

There are probably certain encounters and battles you have faced in the course of your life and you were wondering why you were or still are going through those battles. I'm here to let you know that the devil does not fight against just anybody, but those who he sees as a threat and are opposing him. He fears your influence, he fears what you have the power and potential to accomplish. He wants you to throw in the towel, he wants you to believe this walk is not worth the attacks, but do not give in because greater is He who is in you than he who is in the world. You have the whole of heaven rooting for you and fighting for you, and that is no match for the devil to compete against. The more the Israelites were oppressed, the more they multiplied. Begin to see every attack and battle as an opportunity to excel and level up; what the devil thinks will destroy you will, as a matter of fact, propel you to the level God originally intended for you.

There is a reason for your existence. Before you were born, you were stamped with purpose and you were a threat to the devil. Today, you are still a threat to the

PURPOSE: EXISTED BEFORE EXISTENCE

devil. He may try to take you out and eliminate you but he will not succeed! Your purpose and destiny is too great and powerful for the devil to annihilate.

Now let's look at Jeremiah. Jeremiah was a young man who had been ordained and called as a prophet to the nations by God, not by Facebook, Instagram or people, but God. God made Jeremiah understand that before he was formed in his mother's womb, before his father's sperm met his mother's egg, even before his great grandparents met each other, He knew him and set him apart to be a prophet. He existed as a prophet in the mind and heart of God before coming into physical existence. This was purpose. Such a calling that has been spoken to you directly from God, how can you run away from? However, Jeremiah's response to what God had told him seemed as though he wanted to run away. Jeremiah told God that he cannot speak because he is a youth.

From reading this, we must admit that sometimes we ourselves help the devil to interfere with God's purpose for our lives because we allow our fears, the opinions of people, insecurities and inadequacies to get the best of us. We look at our present selves and think "how? A whole me? I'm not capable of doing that". We look at everything we aren't and forget who the God who called us is. We shouldn't stand in the way of ourselves fulfilling purpose. It is one thing for somebody else to stand in the way of your purpose, but if it is you who is standing in your own way, then it is quite absurd.

There is a particular dream I used to have very frequently. In the dream, my teeth would be loose and they would want to fall out, and because they wanted to come out, I would also help to try and pull it out. But it never would. This was a reoccurring dream I had for years, and I never understood what it meant until I was having a conversation with a friend of mine one day who told me about a dream she had. In her dream, a woman was attempting to pull her teeth out because she had been preaching the gospel of Jesus Christ and was having such a great impact. At that instant, I had an "Aha moment" and finally received an understanding from the Holy Spirit of these dreams I kept on having. My teeth already being loose in the dream made me understand there was already a force at work trying to fight the power vested in my words; because without teeth, you cannot speak. Me helping to pull my teeth out made me understand how I was also limiting myself and the power that lied in my mouth. As a result, trying to pull out my teeth was me stopping myself from speaking, as well as killing the source of my influence and purpose.

PURPOSE: EXISTED BEFORE EXISTENCE

I was standing in the way of myself. I have never been a public speaker, I'm a quiet lady; anytime an opportunity came for me to speak in front of people, I dreaded it! I would be so nervous before the time for me to speak would come. Sometimes, I even turned down the opportunity because I believed speaking was not my thing and that I just COULD NOT speak fluently in front of a huge crowd of people.

I was doing a Moses; focusing on what I couldn't do, rather than what God could do. Sometime after, God caused me to come to the understanding that my insecurities and inadequacies are no match for His grace and power, the very thing which I think is a weakness or a limitation is the very thing He will make use of. His strength is made perfect in our weaknesses; in the areas where we are weak, we are in fact stronger than we think because in those areas is where His grace and strength is made available in abundance.

God in His intentional nature knows why he has called us to do certain things. He never expects us to have it all together because if we did, He knows we wouldn't feel the need or see the significance of relying on Him to do what He requires us to do. A person is always more self-confident in their strengths than their weaknesses. If public speaking was one of my strengths, there is a possibility I would not rely on

God and the Holy Spirit *as much* as I do now whenever I am given the opportunity to speak, preach or teach.

It is God who works in us both to will and to do what pleases Him (Philippians 2:13), so it is God who will ultimately be giving you the ability and capacity to do what He has called you to do. When we limit ourselves, we are limiting the God who works within us; that is something we should NOT do. The fact we existed before existence means God *already* had all things planned out, He simply requires us to follow through with everything He planned.

Remember:

- You existed before you came into existence.
- You were stamped with purpose before you were formed.
- God ordained you to do something; He already knows it, it's time for you to believe it.

Being a Purpose Driven Woman starts with you knowing and believing that you were born on purpose for a purpose.

PURPOSE: EXISTED BEFORE EXISTENCE

***Declaration*:**

Father, I believe that I have a purpose, that you have called and ordained me to do something and fix something in this generation and nation. From now henceforth, I am building my understanding of coming to terms with your purpose for me, that I will not belittle myself nor will I limit myself, but that I will trust your intentional nature. Lord, I declare my life shall be preserved for me to fulfil my God-ordained purpose. In the mighty and powerful name of Jesus Christ, Amen.

"The greatest tragedy in life is not death, but a life without purpose."

- Dr. Myles Munroe

2

"I don't know MY purpose!"

Trying to discover your purpose in life can be one of the most difficult and trying tasks ever. It can cause you to ask so many questions, try out so many different things, or even cause you to remain stagnant because you are just NOT SURE what to do. My life's purpose was something I thought about a lot, and trying to discover my purpose was something I always struggled with.

I remember going through a season of my life after finishing my second year of university whereby I felt as though something was just missing in my existence. I felt lost, I felt confused, and I wasn't sure why I was feeling that way. It was only until after having a conversation with one of my brothers that I realised the reason for my confusion and void: my soul was in pursuit of acquiring God's purpose for my life because I knew after university was when life really began. I hadn't yet finished university, I still had one more year to go, but because I was almost at the end of this phase, my mind kept on fast forwarding to what was going to happen after my season of university had ended. Therefore, as a result of not having any idea of what I was going to do, I was feeling lost and confused, and empty. I had always known I was placed on this earth to do something but I just did not know *what*, and not knowing can be very frustrating at times.

"I DON'T KNOW MY PURPOSE!"

"I don't sing, I don't dance, I'm a quiet person so speaking is DEFINITELY not my thing, I just don't know what I have been called to do". This was my response to every person who ever asked me "what do you think your purpose is?". I never really had any personal long-term aspirations or goals either; in terms of what I would like to do or like to be in the future. I mean *everyone* has a dream of doing something when they grow up: e.g. opening an orphanage, becoming a lawyer, being your own boss, setting up a business, becoming an ordained minister, etc. Not me though, I never had any of those; as if I was a different species. I really used to ask myself whether something was wrong with me and how I couldn't have any long-term aspirations or goals. I honestly did not think it was normal.

"Lord, what have you called me to do??!" were the words consistently on my lips. Being in such a state of uncertainty was not a nice feeling at all, I just wanted to know.

I'm sure God one day concluded that if He doesn't give His daughter a response, this matter will eventually eat her up. He saw how He needed to release what I had created as a burden in my heart. And He did, just at the right time. It was when I finished my final year at university and graduated when He made me realise something and said:

*"discovering your purpose is not necessarily a 'one-day event', but purpose is a journey which you develop in and nurture as you go through life. You won't just stumble into purpose (as if it's a person) one day and start walking in the fulfilment of it. Your life is purpose. You are living purpose. So you may not know exactly what you want to do, you may not have certain aspirations just yet, you may not know MY specific assignments for your life right now, but you must remember that I created everyone's path of life to be different and unique. Not having **any** idea of the specifics of your purpose is not necessarily a bad thing, because you are still on your life's journey to discovering it. So far as you are alive and living, you are on your life's journey to discovering purpose, to discovering the life which I intended for you to live."*

Honestly, at that moment, everything I was worried about was no longer a worry; what was a burden before turned into relief and hope. So, you don't know your purpose? Not to worry, purpose is a journey: a journey to *becoming* who you already are. You won't have it all figured out at once. As you go through the course of your life, it is being revealed and uncovered to you as you go along. Your purpose is not only 'one thing' you will do in your lifetime, but several things because life is purpose and your purpose is made up of different assignments. See it as your own reality TV series which you are living, whereby episode after

"I DON'T KNOW MY PURPOSE!"

episode, something new is being unveiled. You discover more about your purpose day after day if you believe it or not.

God kept this revelation hidden from me and revealed it to me at the appropriate time; because I did not know what exactly to do next after completing my degree, He waited for me to complete the degree first before making me understand that purpose is a journey. Why? He knew that time was the time I needed to hear it the most. The fact I was persistently asking God what to do when the time had not yet come, and when the season was not yet here showed how much I wanted to go ahead of God. I was so concerned about the 'next' when I hadn't even completed the 'now'. God wanted me to focus on what I was doing at that moment, and not distract my focus from what mattered the most at the time: finishing my degree. Maybe you find yourself in a similar predicament; you're in pursuit of knowing more from God about the next but you haven't yet completed the now and you're wondering why God is silent. He wants you to focus on the now and know that He's already in the next season. So when it is time for you to enter the next, you will meet Him there already waiting.

~ Don't Live Somebody Else's Purpose ~

After completing a degree and graduating, the next phase everybody is expecting you to enter is work, finding a job. It's the 'norm', and what we've now become accustomed to; once you finish university, you need to find a job right away, start working and begin earning those coins! You either find a job in the field you studied, or you enter into any field you can find. The latter option is normally as a result of not being able to find a job in your desired field within the time frame you have given yourself, as well as the pressure of the people around you; whether your parents, siblings or general family relatives. Also not forgetting those non-blood related aunties and uncles who without fail constantly ask you whether you have found a job yet anytime they see you, as though they will be receiving a fraction of your salary once you do start working.

I mean, you understand the people around you are simply concerned and care about your circumstance, and are showing a genuine interest; but sometimes it does get a bit too much and the pressure to find a job just builds. Everyone who you graduated with is finding jobs, everyone is earning money and you're at home filling out applications here and there, wondering when a job offer will come through. This was my story.

"I DON'T KNOW MY PURPOSE!"

After graduating, finding a job felt like spiritual warfare. It is even harder when after graduating, you still don't have any idea of what sector or field you would like to enter. After graduating with a degree, I still did not know what I specifically wanted to do. "How could you not know what to do even after completing a degree? If you went to university and chose to study a specific degree, you must have known or had an idea of what you wanted to do" is what I'm sure you are asking. Before starting university, it was my desire to pursue a career in counselling afterwards, hence why I studied Psychology and Counselling. However, as the three years of completing this degree was gradually passing by, this desire slowly began to fade also. Having the opportunity to study counselling made me see how much I did not want to pursue a career in it. I lost interest. As a result, I came out of university more lost than when I entered. So even when looking for jobs, you struggle to know what exactly you should be searching for. This is where the danger of not living your own purpose comes in.

If you do not know what to do, there is a likelihood of you falling into the danger of doing what you are not supposed to do. At that point in my life, there were too many voices in my ear. People were telling me what I should do, where I should go; and so I found myself looking and applying for any and every kind of job. I was going to settle for whatever came my way; forgetting that the danger in settling for anything can lead to deviation from purpose. When you do not know what to do, people will tell you what to do. When you do not know what is good for you, people will decide for you what *they* believe is good for you. People will give you the coat *they* think you should wear, they will give you the words *they* think you should say, and you will find yourself living according to the suggestions and opinions of other people. The pressure of the people has the potential to make you live a life outside of purpose. You will eventually find yourself in foreign nature, living a life that is foreign to God.

I would have found myself entering positions God never really intended for me. God had to remind me that I cannot live anyhow and go wherever the wind blows. Not knowing the specifics of your purpose is not an excuse to do anything and everything. As believers, we do not live a 'try your luck' kind of life whereby you go and try out everything that seems good, hoping to find your fit. God must be our director in everything. The majority of the time, we believe if we enter into something, it could be a job, a relationship, an investment, a business deal, and everything seems to be working out smoothly, then it is okay. If Moses lived life on

"I DON'T KNOW MY PURPOSE!"

his own accord and ended up being anything else other than a deliverer for Israel, he would have failed in life; because that was not the purpose of God for his life. Even if he loved and enjoyed what he was doing and was getting a magnificent salary; he would have been living somebody else's purpose and would have failed to fulfil his own. So many people are living lives God did not purpose them to live and it is a real shame. When I think about a life that is not and has not fulfilled purpose, it honestly saddens me. Previous generations have made this mistake of living life according to their own desires, aspirations and what they thought was good, and have neglected God's perfect will. Just because everything was going according to plan, they thought it was "purpose". Nevertheless, it is my aim through the grace and wisdom of God to make you understand that God's original purpose and will for your life MUST prevail, at all cost! As for this generation and the generations to come, we cannot get it wrong!

For you the situation may differ a little. However, in whatever place you do find yourself, do not end up living somebody else's purpose just because you have not yet discovered the entirety of your own. I had to remember that my life needed to be intentional; even if I had no clue of what I needed to do.

But how do you live an intentional life if you do not know what exactly you need to be intentional about doing?

Keeping your eyes fixed on Jesus. Even when I did not know what to do, there was one thing I knew I *needed* to do; to keep my eyes fixed on the Author and the Finisher of my faith. To keep my focus on Him. We only become confused and overwhelmed with the various issues and matters of life when we allow them to shift our focus from the One who truly matters. It was only when Peter took his eyes off Jesus Christ and focused on the waves that the waves began to consume him. Just as a servant keeps their eyes on their master and a slave girl watches her mistress for the slightest signal (Psalm 123:2), so should it be with us and God. I knew if I kept my eyes fixed on Him, He would cause everything to fall into place and stay in place. These are wise words from one of my sisters that really encouraged me during this season:

> *"the truth is this: it's not that we have it all figured out. It's just that we know we serve a God who before time begun, had all things concerning our lives planned out. We simply put our whole trust in Him alone."*
>
> *-   Angela Sekyere.*

"I DON'T KNOW MY PURPOSE!"

It's okay if you don't have it all figured out just yet, it's okay if you don't know what to do, it's okay if you feel lost and confused. Many people do, you are not the only one. It's better to confess you don't have it all figured out than to confess you do. When you confess that you don't, you are indirectly telling God you NEED Him and cannot do life alone, and according to your own wisdom. You give Him access to establish His plans in your life.

In the next chapters, I am going to share with you everything God taught me and the journey He took me through in my season of unemployment; being lost, jobless and confused. As well as how I found myself living out purpose without even realising. God is going to make you understand through this book that even if you do not know your reason for existence just yet, all hope is not lost. There is a certain life He desires His children to live for them to be purpose driven and live a purposeful life.

I will illuminate in depth what it means to keep your eyes fixed on God, but first, let's look at the importance of laying the right foundation in our pursuit of becoming purpose driven people.

Chapter 3 awaits you…

Prayer:

Abba, sometimes I feel lost and confused in terms of knowing what I need to do in order to fulfil purpose. As purpose is a journey, I pray You will specifically direct my steps in the right direction. May Your light shine on every blurred path for me to follow Your directions clearly. I pray that You will help me to live an intentional life and fulfil my OWN purpose by keeping my eyes fixed on You. In the precious and loving Name of Jesus Christ, Amen.

"*Purpose is a journey, not a one-day event.*"

- Daniella Akosua

3

Laying The Right Foundation

Originating from a country whereby building a house is such a big achievement and accomplishment for the citizens who live there and are from there, I am very much aware of the process, expenses, effort and time needed to build a house. I am of Ghanaian descent, and I have been to Ghana 7 times during my 21 years of life. Of all those 7 times I have travelled to Ghana, without fail, I have had to spend part of my 'holiday' overseeing the construction work being completed in the different sites owned by my parents. I love going to Ghana, but knowing I would have to spend some days at the site just sitting around observing construction made me dread the holiday at the same time; not forgetting those cheeky mosquitoes as well.

There was one particular site we visited very often because it was newly bought, and I remember every time we went there, I would see no changes, no differences. The same grass I would see one year was the same grass I would see the following year. So I asked my mother why it was taking so long to start developing the building, because I mean she has been making me come here year after year, but yet it seems as though my time is being wasted because I don't see any difference or progression. She made me understand there was a lot of work to do for the foundation of the house because there was a lot of water beneath all of the grass and soil, which needed to be removed. A building built on water would be an unstable building. Therefore, a lot of time was spent in making sure the foundation of the building was right before moving on to construct the rest of the building. The foundation of a building is the most important and time-consuming part of construction; if you get the foundation right, the rest of the building will also be right.

Even though there was grass on the land, and all that could be seen was grass, you would think the development of the building was ready to commence. However, it had to take the labouring workers to investigate deeper into the grass to find out there was water below. The grass was a deception. Though there was a harvest, there were still some deeply rooted issues. For that reason, for there to have been a mightier harvest (the building), the deeply rooted issues needed to be tackled and dealt with for the foundation and the building itself to be strong. It took a long time for that process of removing the water to be completed.

Laying the right foundation is not cheap, it is expensive, but it is definitely worth it! In the long run, it will be of great benefit to you because the building is guaranteed to remain firm and steadfast over a long period of time. In our pursuit of becoming purpose driven women, I cannot stress enough the importance of making sure we have laid the correct foundation in order to walk in the full manifestation of who God has created us to be.

The bible emphasises the significance of laying the right foundation in life in Luke 6:47-49 (NKJV):

47 Whoever comes to Me, and hears My sayings and does them, I will show you whom he is like:

48 He is like a man building a house, who dug deep and laid the foundation on the rock. And when the flood arose, the stream beat vehemently against that house, and could not shake it, for it was founded on the rock.

49 But he who heard and did nothing is like a man who built a house on the earth without a foundation, against which the stream beat vehemently; and immediately it fell. And the ruin of that house was great."

The passage of scripture shows Jesus likening a man who hears and is obedient to the word of God to a man who has laid the foundation of a house on rock. When your life is built on the word of God, you ultimately have a strong foundation because rock is strong and steadfast. When you have laid the right foundation in life, you become unmovable and unstoppable. You become a force to be reckoned with. Whatever comes your way, you are able to face it head-on. You are not easily uprooted or beat down, because with the right foundation laid, you become a <u>powerhouse</u>. We are made to understand that Jesus Christ Himself is the Word, the written Word and the living Word (John 1:1-4). As a result, as believers, He is our only foundation (1 Corinthians 3:11), and it is upon this foundation that we continue to build.

    With Jesus Christ being our foundation, it ultimately implies that we must have accepted Him into our lives as our Lord and Saviour. It is a fundamental step to living a purpose driven life because once you have received Christ into your life, you are now made anew (2 Corinthians 5:17) and have literally *given* your life to Him. Some of us have not fully grasped the term 'giving your life to Christ'; we all make the declaration that we have given our lives to Christ, but yet are still holding on to parts of it. When you give your life to Christ, you have given it ALL to Him, withholding nothing. Meaning your life is no longer your own, it has been arrested. It is no longer about you and what you want, but about what He wants and what He requires of you (Galatians 2:20). What He requires of you is to live the life He predestined for you before the beginning of time.

Ephesians 2:8-10 NKJV

8 For by grace you have been saved through faith, and that not of yourselves; it is the gift of God,

9 not of works, lest anyone should boast.

10 For we are His workmanship, created in Christ Jesus for good works, which God prepared beforehand that we should walk in them.

This passage of scripture is quite a popular one; when most people receive salvation, it is what they are continuously taught. They are taught how they did not have to do anything to receive salvation, it is a free gift which is available to everyone to receive. All we had to do was confess with our mouths and believe in our hearts and we would be saved. This was drummed into our heads from the very moment we received salvation; which is the absolute truth. Surprisingly, from the many times I have heard teachings on this passage of scripture, it seems as though the verse 10 is invisible, it is hardly ever included. The focus is mainly on the two verses prior: that we have been saved and that it is not our right to boast in that fact, but the reason as to *why* we were saved is hardly ever spoken about.

The definition of the word *"for"* is *'to be in support of or in favour of'*, or *'because of or as a result of something'*.

LAYING THE RIGHT FOUNDATION

Therefore, having verse 10 start with the word *"for"* shows us it is a continuation and a supporting statement of the two verses aforementioned. As a result of us or because of the fact we were saved by grace through faith, we *are* His workmanship, created to do good works. We were not saved for the simple fact that God just wanted to save us and spend eternity with us. Although it is a crucial factor, there is more! Verse 10 is the fruit or the evidence of verses 8 and 9, it is what must be testified of us as a result of receiving salvation! I love the way the Amplified translation puts it:

10 For we are His workmanship [His own master work, a work of art], created in Christ Jesus [reborn from above—spiritually transformed, renewed, ready to be used] for good works, which God prepared [for us] beforehand [taking paths which He set], so that we would walk in them [living the good life which He prearranged and made ready for us].

This scripture plainly talks about being ordained before existence too. You did not lay the foundation of accepting Christ into your life just so you could have something to say, sit around looking pretty and live a normal, mediocre life. No. Once you have laid this foundation, there is more to do, the construction work must continue; you must be ready and willing to be used to carry out the good works He prepared beforehand; walking along the paths He set out before you prior to your birth. That is why I was saved. That is why you were saved.

However, it is all good and well knowing we have laid a foundation to continue building on it; and by building on it, I am referring to you pursuing the life God initially prepared for you. On the other hand, it is also important to realise and come to terms with the reality that many of us have laid our foundation, and have begun building on it but have neglected the fact there were some deeply rooted issues that needed to be dealt with. Remember the water that needed to be dealt with before the building could continue to be built? There was still grass; in other words, there was still growth, there was still progression, there was still development, but the greater growth and development could not occur if the water was not dealt with. And the truth of the matter is, as much as we build, as much as we determine in our hearts to live a purpose driven life, there will come a time where we would not be able to neglect those deeply rooted issues any longer. We will still need to go back to some of these issues we have buried in order for our growth, our progression and development to be stable and unwavering. They could be emotional, spiritual, social or physical.

When we look at the life of Apostle Paul, and the beginning of his journey as a born again believer, there is something we can learn. After Paul had his encounter with Jesus, regained his sight, got baptised and filled with the Holy Spirit, Acts chapter 9 makes us understand how he stayed with the believers in Damascus for some time and even began preaching. He then went back to Jerusalem after staying in Arabia for 3 years and tried very much to unite with the believers there, and eventually started to travel with the apostles preaching boldly in the name of Jesus. However, this did not go so well. In verse 29 of chapter 9, we see how Paul finds himself in a testing situation. He finds himself disputing and arguing with a group of Greek-speaking Jews. The 'argumentative Paul' that argued and fought with the believers before his conversion had not yet been dealt with. Paul was not entirely ready to go out and preach just yet, he still had some deeply rooted issues to deal with: his argumentative character. Even though he was moving with the other believers and apostles, he still had some work to do on himself. As a result, the apostles decided to send him back to Tarsus, his hometown, back to where it all started.

Funnily enough, when Paul was no longer there, the bible records there was sudden peace in the churches; the churches were developed and strengthened in faith, and they began to multiply. This goes to show that if you do not deal with the deeply rooted issues before doing what God has called you to do, you become a detriment to those around you. When you think you are trying to help them, you are in fact harming them. Paul became a detriment to the believers in Jerusalem even though he had received salvation and had spent 3 years of solitude in Arabia before going to Jerusalem (Galatians 1:17), and so had to be sent away.

So for some of us, we have built upon the foundation, but are still struggling to remain steadfast and strong because we have not been built on stable ground. This is why sometimes we may find ourselves making progress, but then regressing again after some time. You may be thinking that if you have laid the right foundation by accepting Jesus Christ into your life, then all should be well. However, there will come a time where these issues will begin to creek through the foundation and become evident in your personality, character, thoughts, speech, etc., whether consciously or subconsciously, and will ultimately have an effect on your life and relationships. They won't stay hidden for long.

I do realise it is not entirely our fault for having laid the foundation of salvation first before dealing with root issues, because the truth is, most of the time, they only come to light once we *have* received Christ into our lives. The most important thing is that once they do, we *must* deal with them appropriately. I will tackle laying the right foundation from 3 angles: identity, self-love and emotional healing.

~ **Identity Breeds Purpose** ~

One battle every generation of young people face is the battle of *'identity'*, embracing and accepting their true identity.

- ❖ A woman of purpose must know who she is.
- ❖ A woman of purpose must be unapologetic about who she is.

You will struggle to live a purpose driven life if you are blind to who you are and are not willing to accept who you truly are. Likewise, it is also important to make sure that the identity you believe about yourself is true, sincere and in accordance with the word of God.

For a long time, I used to (and still do) call myself the Apple of God's Eye. From the time I attached this identity to myself, I didn't know what it truly meant to be the Apple of God's Eye. I just liked the sound of it and so attached the name to myself. On the other hand, at the same time when I was young, naïve, and in secondary school, I had another tag name—Lady Skrewface. I give you permission to laugh. I still laugh today when I think about it. These were two names I associated with myself which were the complete opposite of each other to birth my identity; what a contradiction. Imagine the spiritual battles they were having to determine my identity, and eventually my life.

The identity you attach to yourself will eventually decide the course of your life, and that is the absolute truth. Names are very powerful and must not be taken lightly. I honestly remember when I attached the tag name Lady Skrewface to my life, even though I already had a fixed screw face (mercy), my face remained screwed, my attitude began to change, I would be angry for no reason, sometimes I would be upset for no reason. I always had people asking me: "why are you so upset?" and "why do you always look angry?". Even strangers on the street would approach me and tell me to smile. That made me even more annoyed to be very honest. At the time I did not understand why, but looking back, I understand. Identity really does breed purpose! This identity began to determine how I lived and behaved, even though there were other causes that contributed to my behaviour.

LAYING THE RIGHT FOUNDATION

When we look at the life of Jacob in the book of Genesis, the guy literally lived according to the identity given to him by his name. The name Jacob means "trickster" or "deceiver"; so you can imagine the kind of life he lived. Even from the time he came out of his mother's womb and was seen grabbing the heel of his brother, you knew this son will be a troublesome one. He was deceitful, so much so that he blackmailed his own brother, Esau, into selling his birth-right to him, as well as deceiving his father into thinking he was Esau to receive the fatherly blessing. It was an identity, but an identity that was not in alignment with the mind of God. Hence why God changed his name to Israel; His chosen nation, His beloved people; the lineage which His Son Jesus Christ would come from. What this teaches is: there must be a certain identity you carry and believe about yourself in order for certain things to be birthed from you, both spiritually and physically. You cannot believe you are a failure and expect to birth success. You cannot believe you are shy and expect to be speak boldly in front of people. Jacob's identity needed to be changed in order for Jesus Christ to have come from that lineage; for Jacob's later generations to be great, blessed and significant in history. That is the power of identity.

I'm reminded of a story of a female mentor and her female mentee who was facing and going through a whole lot of struggles, issues, and problems. One of the issues the mentee was going through involved false rumours being spread around about her. She had found herself in an incident which eventually got exposed, and the truth of the story got twisted in some way. People were calling her names, spreading the things she had done without knowing the whole truth behind the real story, lying on her and a whole lot more. It was a very distressing time for this young lady. She couldn't handle it.

With all the counsel her mentor was giving her, it was as though the words of her mentor were going in one ear and out of the other, her words were literally hitting a brick wall. The mentee was so consumed with what everybody else was saying about her that the words of her mentor became empty words. She started to believe and accept the words spoken by the rumour spreaders. She began to accept it as truth and accept it *was her identity*. She allowed people to tell her who she was rather than telling herself who she was. She allowed people to shape her identity rather than shaping her own identity. Sadly, this is what happens when you do not know who you are and whose you are. When you know who you are, the words of other people will have no chance to cultivate your identity. People will always try to give you an identity, whether positively and negatively, but what you do not do is allow their words to shape you as a person. If you don't place the right identity upon yourself, you give other people the license to do so. Nobody knows who you truly are except for God. Do not become a product of the words and identity other people place upon you.

Establish your identity before somebody establishes it for you. It may not necessarily be a specific name, but it could simply be the way you see yourself, the way you talk to yourself, what you confess about yourself. What you confess about yourself will eventually begin to take form in your life. Why? Because words carry power (Proverbs 18:21).

Begin to identify what the word of God says about you and what God thinks of you. There are many passages of scripture which tell you the identity He has given you as His child, and here are a few to get you started in believing the correct identity about yourself:

Genesis 1:27 (NKJV) – You are God's Creation.

> 27 So God created man in His own image; in the image of God He created him; male and female He created them.

Psalm 8:3-4 (NKJV) – You are Cherished.

> *3 When I consider Your heavens, the work of Your fingers,*
> *The moon and the stars, which You have ordained,*
> *4 What is man that You are mindful of him,*
> *And the son of man that You visit him?*

Psalm 139:14-15 (NKJV) – You are God's Masterpiece.

> *14 I will praise You, for I am fearfully and wonderfully made;*
> *Marvellous are Your works,*
> *And that my soul knows very well.*
> *15 My frame was not hidden from You,*
> *When I was made in secret,*
> *And skilfully wrought in the lowest parts of the earth.*

Song of Solomon 4:7 (AMP) – You are Beautiful.

> *7 "O my love, you are altogether beautiful and fair.*
> *There is no flaw nor blemish in you!*

LAYING THE RIGHT FOUNDATION

John 1:12 (NKJV) – You are a Child of God.

12 But as many as received Him, to them He gave the right to become children of God, to those who believe in His name.

John 15:15 (NKJV) – You are a Friend of Jesus.

15 No longer do I call you servants, for a servant does not know what his master is doing; but I have called you friends, for all things that I heard from My Father I have made known to you.

Romans 8:17 (NKJV) – You are Royalty.

17 and if children, then heirs—heirs of God and joint heirs with Christ, if indeed we suffer with Him, that we may also be glorified together.

Ephesians 2:19 (NKJV) – You are a Citizen of the Kingdom.

19 Now, therefore, you are no longer strangers and foreigners, but fellow citizens with the saints and members of the household of God.

1 Peter 2:9 (NKJV) – You are Set Apart and Chosen.

9 But you are a chosen generation, a royal priesthood, a holy nation, His own special people, that you may proclaim the praises of Him who called you out of darkness into His marvellous light;

1 John 3:1a (NKJV) – You are Loved.

> *Behold what manner of love the Father has bestowed on us, that we should be called children of God!*

One thing I began to do, something I learnt from my youth president, was to make 'I AM…' declarations about myself. I would write down what I believed the word of God said about me and what I believe God says about me *personally* in my journal. I would encourage you to do the same. As you consistently read over it and meditate upon it, you will eventually begin to see those words and declarations manifest in your life.

Life becomes purposeful when you know who you truly are and are confident in who you are. When you begin to discover and learn more about yourself, you ultimately begin to learn and discover more about your life's purpose. John the Baptist knew who he truly was when he was asked by the Pharisees to reveal his identity, and so was able to answer their question appropriately. He made a bold 'I AM' statement and confessed in John 1:23 (NKJV):

> [23] *He said: "I am*
>
> *'The voice of one crying in the wilderness:*
> *"Make straight the way of the* LORD*,".*

He was able to declare boldly that he wasn't the Christ simply because he knew his *own* identity. Knowing who you are will cause you to know the distinctiveness of your purpose. The people came and asked him this question because they saw that the identity and purpose of John and the identity and purpose which was prophesied about the Christ were very much similar. However, John was able to make a distinction between his own identity and purpose, and the identity and purpose of Jesus Christ. He baptised with water, but Jesus Christ baptised with the Holy Spirit. You must know who you are so that you do not fall into the danger of thinking and believing you are somebody or something you are not. Knowing your true identity opens the door to living the life God preordained for *you*. John the Baptist did not feel intimidated by the ministry and purpose of Jesus Christ because he was **grounded in his identity**; he knew what he had been called to do and so did exactly that. He stayed in his lane because he knew who he was.

The reason why many of us struggle to stay in our lane and begin to feel intimated by others when we see they are beginning to walk in their purpose is because of a lack of identity. When we begin to feel intimidated, we start playing the *'comparison game'*. That's when we start comparing ourselves to others, measuring our progress against the progress of others and living according to the standards other people have set for themselves. That is not the life God desires His children to live. He desires His children to know their real identity in order for them to live according to His standards for their lives.

On the other hand, many of us know our identity or believe certain identities about ourselves but do not truly understand what it means to carry that identity. It's one thing to know, but it's another thing to understand. Not understanding your identity will prevent you from walking in the full power and authority of it. Do not let that be you.

There is a valuable lesson we can learn from our mother of all creation: Eve. Eve had the ability to operate in the full authority and power of her identity but didn't because she was not fully grounded in it. This is why she allowed herself to be deceived and tricked into eating from the tree of knowledge of good and evil. The serpent said to her after asking whether God truly instructed them not to eat from the tree: *"For God knows that in the day you eat of it your eyes will be opened, and **you will be like God**, knowing good and evil."* (Genesis 3:5 NKJV). I place an emphasis on the fact he said *"and you will be like God"*. Eve was already like God! Why? Because she was made in His image and in His likeness. That was her identity. What she already was, the serpent was able to make her believe she wasn't, simply because she did not fully understand. She had the power and authority to shun the lie of the serpent, but the serpent took advantage of her ignorance.

Because I know I am the Apple of God's Eye, I believe and understand that I AM recklessly loved, with an unfailing love. I understand that I AM precious to Him, I AM dear to His heart, I AM protected, that I AM cared for by Him and that His eyes are CONTINUALLY upon me. Anytime I lift myself up in prayer to God, I let the devil know I am **untouchable** because I AM the Apple of God's Eye.

Understand who you are. It is only until you have the understanding that you will become confident and grounded in it, whereby nobody will be able to tell you otherwise. If you call yourself a Woman of Influence, study and search what it means to actually be a Woman of Influence; study and look at women who were influential in the bible, as well as women who are influential around us today. How does somebody who calls them self a Woman of Influence live, talk and behave? A Purpose Driven Woman must establish the correct identity and be confident in it.

~ Self Love ~

The topic of self-love is a topic I have noticed is seldom ever spoken about amongst believers. We talk about what it means and the importance of loving God and loving others, but leave out the importance of loving ourselves. This is the reason why we find a lot of people, especially believers, who struggle to truly and genuinely love themselves; sometimes without even realising. Self-love ties in very much with identity. Many of us struggle with self-love because we are not rooted in our identity. Self-love can only be implemented when you see yourself the way God does. My personal definition of self-love is *"agreeing with God to see yourself the way He sees you; seeing eye to eye with God; seeing God in the reflection of your mirror."*

A Purpose Driven Woman must love herself, and her love for herself must stem from the love God has for her. That is the only way she can *genuinely* love herself. Some of us struggle with self-love as a result of many reasons: our weight, our skin, our hair, our facial features, our bodily features, emotional abuse, physical abuse, sexual abuse, criticisms, comparison, even some of our mistakes. Due to some of the mistakes we made in our lifetime, we fail to forgive ourselves for what we did, and as a result, fail to love ourselves again. And many of these factors have the potential to lead to insecurities, low self-esteem, emotional wounds, feelings of worthlessness, lack of confidence and so much more.

As a child of God, as a daughter of God, I want you to know that *you are enough.*

You are beautiful. You are flawless. You are recklessly loved by the One who is love. You were created uniquely, you were handcrafted with care and precision. Nothing about you is a mistake and nothing about you is flawed. Everything about you is intentional.

Self-love begins with knowing and embracing God's love. Once you are able to agree with God's thoughts about you, you are able to accept you for you. Do not restrict yourself from receiving the love of God because you are angry at yourself. Do not feel as though you are unworthy of receiving God's love. We are made to understand that nothing, absolutely nothing can separate us from the love of God (Romans 8:38-39). If you struggle with self-love, it is most likely because you have not really encountered the love God has for you. A prayer that must be prayed is:

"God, overwhelm me with Your love."

It is a very simple prayer, but from the day I began praying this prayer, I cried a pool of tears in my room. His love overwhelmed my heart so much; I just could not comprehend it. His love showed me it has the ability to override all guilt, insecurities, and shame. I struggled with self-love and I didn't even know it. I always found myself complaining about features I didn't like about myself or wasn't so fond of. I thought it was normal; I knew everyone had something about themselves they didn't like. However, when that thing becomes an insecurity whereby you begin to do things which result in you covering up or hiding those features, it develops into a lack of self-love.

For a very long time, one thing I never did was smile with my teeth. I have a front gap tooth and I used to HATE it. I thought it was ugly, I thought it was unattractive; I just did not like it. It became such a big insecurity for me. People would always say to me *"Daniella, your gap is not even that big"*, but they didn't understand. Insecurities are deeply rooted issues you won't understand unless you are dealing with them. Anytime I would laugh, without fail, I would cover my mouth. Covering my mouth became so much of a habit that I began to do it subconsciously. To me, society placed such a big emphasis on having perfect, straight teeth and would make you feel some way if you didn't. The jokes

I would hear about gap teeth's, the memes I would see, I just wanted straight teeth. It was only until someone mentioned to me how they have never seen me smile with my teeth, and began to encourage me when I told them why that I was really challenged to overcome this insecurity. I took it before God in prayer and He really did begin working on me from within to accept my 'flaw'. Opinions of others cannot dictate how we feel about ourselves. That's bondage. How we see ourselves and feel about ourselves should be a reflection of how God sees us and feels about us. That's self-love.

One thing that has deceived some of us when it comes to self-love is thinking that self-love is based on the confidence you have in your outward appearance and features. People mistake self-love for having nothing to be ashamed of in their public appearance simply because everything is the way they want it. For some of us, it is based on the vain love we have for ourselves. We must know the difference between self-love and vanity so we do not deceive ourselves. Wise words from the mother of King Lemuel about the Proverbs 31 woman:

> *30 Charm is deceitful and beauty is passing,*
> *But a woman who fears the Lord, she shall be praised.*

This clearly makes us understand that outward appearance can be misleading; it is not our outward appearance that makes us women of beauty, substance, and virtue, but it is a soul that reverences, acknowledges and respects God. And a woman who ultimately respects the Lord from within will ultimately respect His creation and handiwork. Do not claim to be a Proverbs 31 woman or a 1 Peter 3 woman if you place beauty solely on external things; these women understand that beauty starts from within. 1 Peter 3:4 makes it clear that a *gentle and quiet spirit* is what God classifies as true beauty, true beauty which never fades. It is what's on the inside that matters!

Self-love is an internal decision which then extends to the external. So even if you do love everything feature of yourself, you love it simply because you know God loves your features as they are too. You cannot truly love yourself if you don't understand the love God has for you. God looks past your "insecurities" and "flaws" and loves you for YOU. David said, *"I will praise You, for I am fearfully and wonderfully made; Marvellous are Your works, and that my soul knows very well."* (Psalms 139:14 NKJV). He was confident and bold in agreeing with and accepting God's creation; not just externally but internally. He says "his soul knows very well"; does your soul believe you are fearfully and wonderfully made? It must! You are God's handiwork, His masterpiece, and He makes NO mistakes. Begin to look past your insecurities and see eye to eye with God, see Him in the reflection of your mirror.

There may be quite a few things you may not like about yourself, I pray He begins to overwhelm your heart with His love so you will begin to see yourself through His lens and love you for you. Whatever it may be, it could be something really small you did not even notice you disliked, take it to Him in prayer and ask Him to release you from those insecurities. You cannot be a PDW and still nurse insecurities. We must break loose.

~ Emotional Healing ~

When you study yourself as a person, the way you behave, the way you speak, the way you think, the way you reason, the way you carry yourself, your personality and your characteristics, it will come to your attention that people are not the way they are simply because that's just "the way they are". Studying Psychology and Counselling as a degree helped me to understand this more than I did before as well, *especially* concerning myself (at least my degree was beneficial to some extent). Realising this is essentially what inspired the topic for my dissertation in my final year: 'The

Effects of Childhood Attachment and Parental Separation on Adult Attachment and Personality'. There is always an explanation for people's behaviour and emotions. The majority of the time, it is as a result of past experiences that have the potential to create emotional wounds.

There was a season in my life where God began dealing with me about my emotional wounds. The emotional wounds I had buried for a very long time. I always knew there were certain characteristics and personality traits I possessed which were "not me"; I knew they were as a result of things I had experienced and encountered in life. However, I always thought I could keep those wounds buried; I always thought I could keep those experiences buried, I always thought I could keep those root issues, those seeds which were sown and the manifestation of those seeds buried. I thought they wouldn't have that much of an effect on me as I grew in Christ. I thought I could just forget about them and live on. Nonetheless, God began dealing with me and made me understand that for Him to take me to the places He has destined for me, I need to come face to face with myself and deal with these wounds I had buried for years. It is the same again with the water that was beneath the grass. No matter how much I would try to build, I would still have to go back to the roots.

LAYING THE RIGHT FOUNDATION

~ A Purpose Driven Woman cannot FULLY fulfil her God-ordained purpose if she is still covering and hiding emotional wounds ~

As women in general, we are very emotional beings. You don't even need statistics to tell you that, if you are a woman indeed, you will know it is the truth. Therefore, there are many experiences we will encounter in life that will affect us emotionally, whether we choose to agree or not. When God was prepping me for the writing of this book and made me understand I would have to be very transparent in this section, I honestly did not think I could do it. I was scared; with tears in my eyes and snot in my nose, I confessed to Him that it would be very hard. Sadly, my tears didn't change His mind but rather He continued to challenge me to be very real and raw simply because of the power that lies in being transparent. My transparency has the ability to bring about healing and deliverance; that is what God made me understand. I had to think about the souls this would help and encourage, rather than myself.

When God was taking me through my journey of emotional healing, He opened my eyes to many things, things I honestly struggled to accept and admit. I wanted to be healed, I wanted to be delivered, I wanted to be set free from those wounds, but it was imperative I was true to myself about what had affected me and how it affected me. In our pursuit to becoming Purpose Driven Women, if we sincerely want to be set free from emotional bondage, we must be willing to accept and admit the root causes of what actually wounded us, the seeds those root causes sowed in us and the actions those seeds caused us to take.

There is a term I have heard quite frequently which is "Purpose in Pain". There is always a greater purpose in the pain we have experienced in life, but it is down to us to find the courage to be willing to identify that purpose. There cannot be purpose in your pain if you are not willing to acknowledge and embrace your pain. God desires to use your pain to birth purpose, but He cannot do that if you are hiding it. God cannot heal what you aren't willing to expose.

There was a time prior to this period whereby one of my sisters, who is also like a mentor to me, asked me a question, and the question went like this: "who is Daniella?". When she first asked me the question, I was confused and asked her if she actually wanted me to give an answer. She said yes, and also told me to take some time to look at myself in the mirror and write down what I see. I did exactly that. I remember looking at myself in the mirror and crying. There were so many things I could see that represented brokenness, hurt, confusion; and coming to that realisation was hard, so I stopped and left it there. I didn't want to come face to face with myself at the time, exposing those things to *myself* felt uncomfortable. I did not want to admit and accept it, but root issues will always be root issues that need to be confronted.

A woman who is still covering and hiding emotional wounds is a woman who is holding herself back and preventing her FULL potential from being released. To walk in the full manifestation of who you are, you must give God ALL of you, not only the parts of you that look pretty. God must be given access to work on *all* of you, not only the parts that you are *comfortable* with Him working on.

The pain of everything you have experienced wasn't permanent, it was temporary. You will realise it was only there to show you that something, which was worth the pain, had the potential to be birthed. A mother who cries out in labour pains to give birth understands that the pain is necessary, because at the end of all the pain, the birth of the child will bring great joy and fulfilment, and it would have been well worth it. In spiritual terms, our birth isn't a baby, but purpose. Allow God to birth purpose from your pain.

My emotional healing journey began with God taking me through a process of revealing my true emotions to myself, and causing me to write everything down for me to literally come face to face with myself. This time I could not run away because I came to understand that if I did, I would essentially be running away from fulfilling purpose.

---------------- ---------------- ---------------- ----------------

I was insecure. I had trust issues. I was bitter. I was fearful. I was doubtful. I was lost. I was confused. I had a fear of rejection. I had a fear of being used (not trusting people's intentions). I had a lack of self-acceptance. I felt unappreciated. I had a lack of self-love. I struggled with comparison. I struggled to express my true emotions and feelings. I was discontent. I always felt like a victim. I wanted to be loved and desired. I had mood swings. I battled with evil and perverse thoughts. I struggled with lust. I was over-possessive. I was proud. I struggled with inner loneliness. I was jealous. I struggled to show and receive affection. I struggled with people bondage.

I was broken.

God took me through this phase of brokenness in order for me to be mended.

LAYING THE RIGHT FOUNDATION

These were all the seeds that had been planted in me from the root causes, as well as the manifestation of these seeds. After God took me through the process of revealing my true emotions, He then took me through the process of revealing the root issues. These root issues consisted of the separation of my parents when I was young, not having a close relationship with my dad, being sexually manipulated at a young age, not being exposed to healthy love and relationships, not receiving enough affection and attention from the right people as a child, broken family bonds, fake friends, never really having one best friend, my weight always being commented on, poor friendship cycles and more. When going through this journey, there was a formula that God made me understand had been operating.

Root Issues → Seeds → Manifestation of Seed

For instance, being sexually manipulated (being used to satisfy somebody else's sexual feelings and desires, and allowing it because of my naivety and ignorance at such a young age) was a root cause. This is one thing that took me a while to accept. I vowed I would take this to the grave and that I would never mention this to anyone, especially my family; considering the manipulation was by a close family friend. Sexual manipulation/exploitation is always an issue that is hard to accept, because such issues cause you to feel vulnerable in the eyes of others, and I mean who likes to feel vulnerable? No one. So many people struggle to voice out their negative sexual experiences because they feel ashamed; I found it shameful how I could have been so naïve to allow such a thing to happen regardless of how old I was. But that is only a tactic the enemy uses to keep us in fear and bondage. Having been sexually manipulated is **not** embarrassing, nor does it mean you are weak. The fact you are still alive shows you are a victor, not a victim; because it did not defeat you, you still have the ability to defeat it and its effects.

The seeds this incident sowed in me was the seed of lust, having trust issues and having a fear of being used. The manifestation of these seeds were having my first boyfriend at the age of 13, involving myself in lustful activities with people until the age of 16, watching erotic and sexual shows in my early secondary school years, always thinking people had hidden intentions when they would try to get close to me, and having a reserved personality. I always thought being reserved was just a personality trait of mine until God made me realise during this journey that it was simply a defence mechanism and a method of building walls of 'safety' and 'protection' to keep people from coming in and knowing the real me.

My parents' separation affected me more than I even knew. From the time my parents separated when I was young, I became withdrawn as the years went by. I was always in my room, I always wanted to be alone if I was at home, I became quieter as a person, I would attend events and return home in the A.M.'s. At the time, I didn't realise what was happening. With so much going on at the time, feelings of rejection began to creep in. I'm not receiving the attention I need, and I'm not receiving the affection that I need. I wanted love and affection, but at the same time wanted to be alone and was fearful of receiving the love and attention as a result of other incidents. I wanted, but did not know how to receive what I wanted.

A lady who did not receive enough love and attention from her parents as a child will ultimately go and search for that love and affection elsewhere when she grows older. If she is able to find what she is looking for, she will remain there; with a high possibility that her immature emotions will be taken for granted purely because she does not know how to receive what she was looking for *properly*.

I'm a daddy's girl. However, not having the opportunity to develop a closer bond with my dad as I grew older was not beneficial to me. Fathers, and even brothers, play a very important role in showing their daughters/sisters how they should be loved. If a father isn't there to do so, that daughter will not know how she is supposed to be loved and will end up entertaining useless and unserious boys; trying to fill a void with the wrong kind of attention. The responsibility a father was supposed to have, some vagabond boy will end up taking that responsibility and give the daughter a falsified perspective on how they should be treated. I always entertained the attention of guys because it was attention I hardly ever received. Yet, I still had a guard up because of the seeds of fear (which looking back was an advantage for me in those situations; see how all things really do work together, haha). However, it was an emotional mess; what you would call emotional dysfunction, I did not know how to regulate my emotions.

During the times I would involve myself in some of these activities and portray certain attitudes, I remember moments where I would do them, ask God for forgiveness and promise to never do them again. But when the devil knows your weakness, he will always try and bring about people and situations that have the potential to make you fall. For example, I had not involved myself in lustful activities since the age of 16, and because of that, I thought things were well. Throughout this journey, God brought to my attention that the only reason why I think I'm fine is because I have not found myself in such situations since; but the seed is still there. So if a situation is to come my way, there is a possibility I still may fall. I had to go through a process of uprooting and deliverance. God said, "all the seeds need to be uprooted". When the seeds are uprooted, the root issues will have no power over you any longer. The root issues will still be there; you will still remember them but they won't have any authority. See the seeds as the power supply of the root issues; once the power supply has been cut off, they have no power, they have nothing to fuel them. It's time to uproot.

God desires His children to be emotionally healed, emotionally stable and emotionally whole, and this can only be done with His help and with the help of the Holy Spirit. Many of us have emotional wounds; some of us know, some of us know but are ignoring them, and some of us have simply become numb to them. The worst thing is to know and not do anything about it; a wound that is not treated appropriately will end up becoming worse and will have the potential to affect other parts of the body.

Not dealing with emotional wounds will eventually give you a distorted view of certain things in life. That is one thing I realised. Emotional wounds cause you to perceive things in a way they aren't at all. For instance, I would consider myself to be a prophetic person; knowing the mind of God concerning situations, people, myself, etc. However, being a prophetic person and having trust issues will basically equal to confusion. A person with trust issues will already have problems trusting people, but because they are also a prophetic person, there is a possibility they'll deceive themselves into thinking their 'prophetic senses' are telling them to not get close to a particular person, when in fact it is just their trust issues coming into play. An emotionally wounded person will take offense in anything and everything, when there was nothing to even be offended about. They will think every shot thrown was aimed at them, even though no shots have been thrown. This is why it will be difficult to fully function as a Purpose Driven Woman if emotional wounds are still untreated.

God also desires you to be transparent, especially to Him. I have not mentioned all of these things simply because I want to expose myself, but because I want to encourage you to do the same. Transparency is the best teacher. I want to encourage you and let you know you can be set free, you can be healed and you can be delivered. You don't have to struggle any longer, you don't have to blame yourself any longer, you don't have to put on a mask any longer. Sometimes we become so used to putting on a mask before people, we forget to take it off when we go before God. Some

LAYING THE RIGHT FOUNDATION

of us have subconsciously been trained to be ashamed of being transparent for various reasons. For myself, I would say because of my background. Coming from a background such as mine; the word transparency is a foreign word, so you are ultimately forced to keep and hold certain things on the inside of you, simply because it is something you are not exposed to.

However, that shouldn't stop you from going before God unashamed and transparently, confidently and truthfully, laying out all your concerns before Him. Acknowledging you are not okay and perfect, and as a result, need Him to heal you, need Him to work on you, need Him to prune you. God knows it all, but He just wants to see you acknowledge these things and hear it from your mouth. God is a FATHER; ready and willing to grab you, His daughter, into His gracious and loving arms. He is ready to take away the garment of sin and shame, and clothe you with the garment of righteousness and glory.

If you believe you need to go on an emotional healing journey; on the next two pages is the step by step process God took me through which you could use as a guide.

1. Get yourself into a place/space of quiet and solitude (you may wish to play an instrumental in the background).
2. Ask God to help you to come face to face with yourself, to be honest with yourself in terms of identifying your true emotions and feelings (the seeds). Once He begins to reveal them, write them down.
3. Write down the manifestations (the things you may have done as a result of the seeds). It may be hard to accept some of the things you did, but it's the only way to move forward. And if you can, try and link the manifestations directly to the seeds which you think were the cause.
4. Now the root issues; you may know some of the root issues by memory. But still ask God to bring to your memory anything you have encountered which you may have forgotten about. Write these down also.
5. Once you have identified the root issues, the seeds, and the manifestations, take it to God in prayer.
    - ➢ First of all, ask Him to give you a heart of humility that can come before Him transparently and raw (1 Peter 5:7; Psalm 51:10; Isaiah 57:15).

- Ask Him to forgive you of anything you may have done (1 John 1:9).
- Ask Him to uproot every negative and ungodly seed that has been planted in you, and ask Him to deliver you and set you free from the bondage of those seeds (Matthew 15:13; John 8:36).
- Ask Him to bring healing and restoration to your soul (Psalm 147:3; Jeremiah 30:17); that He clothes you with a new garment and His glory (Isaiah 61:3). Also, that He helps you to forgive those who may have caused the wounds (Mark 11:25).

6. Daily, ask the Holy Spirit to be the regulator of your emotions; to control them and guide you in knowing how to respond and react to situations and circumstances (Romans 8:14).

This is a very general and brief guide, there may be a lot more things you will do subjective to your experiences. Depending on the severity of the seeds, you may see it necessary to go on your emotional healing journey with an accountability partner or spiritual father/mother. I would always do check-ins with my accountability partners when I was going through this journey just so somebody was aware and could support and encourage me if I ever felt like giving up. It can get to that point, whereby you feel as though the healing process is overwhelming. Just do not go on this journey alone; there is a reason why God has placed people around us (Proverbs 15:22; 24:6). Especially seeing as this topic is a very sensitive and emotional topic, it is best that at least one person is aware.

Whilst on this journey, never allow the voice of condemnation to keep you down. The accuser of the brethren will always try to make you stay feeling guilty of what you may have done. However, once all unrighteousness, ungodliness, and unholiness has been confessed to God and forgiven by Him, you are no longer associated with them. You have been justified. God no longer holds it against you, therefore you should no longer hold it against yourself nor allow the devil to hold it against you. Condemnation will be the loudest voice in your ear if you do not go to Jesus. The woman caught in the act of adultery in John 8 was marked guilty in the midst of the accusers, and I'm sure she also felt guilty. When it was just left with her and Jesus alone, she was forgiven and I'm sure she also felt forgiven and justified. The accusers will always be there to accuse and condemn, but when you go to Jesus and it is just you and HIM, all condemnation ceases and all judgement is null and void. The condemners themselves are the ones who even brought her to her freedom and forgiveness; they worked in her favour. You must go to Jesus, one on one in order to flee from the presence of your accusers, otherwise you will forever feel condemned. *"Who shall bring a charge against God's elect? It is God who justifies"* (Romans 8:33). Once you have been justified by God, nobody can bring you on trial again. When I think of the things I used to do and look at my life now and how God is even using me to write this book, I get confused. I say to myself "this God doesn't make sense". The way He loves and the way He justifies is unfair, and it doesn't make sense! But this is the kind of God we serve! He keeps no record of wrongs, loves unconditionally, and transforms the lives of the 'worst'.

A Purpose Driven Woman is a woman who KNOWS that she has been justified by Christ and that her past mistakes cannot keep her down or hold her hostage. She is a woman who purposes in her heart to know her true identity, understand self-love and be emotionally whole. She is a woman who understands that everything she went through and encountered in life only came to birth purpose.

Prayer:

Heavenly Father, I pray for grace, I pray for strength and I pray for courage to lay the right foundation in life. Even as I purpose in my heart to lay the right foundation, help me to identify areas in my life that must be dealt with and transformed for my foundation to be strong and steadfast. And as You do that, may your Holy Spirit guide me through the process of making sure the right foundation is laid at the end of it all. In the Merciful Name of Jesus Christ, I pray, Amen.

"When the root is deep, there is no reason to fear the wind."

- African Proverb

4

God says:

"Walk with Me…"

I was getting married, but to the wrong person! It was like an arranged marriage; I only found out who the guy was on the day of the wedding. Everyone was saying "yes Daniella, he is the one", but deep down I KNEW he was NOT the one. I knew I was about to make the biggest mistake of my life. Nothing at the wedding seemed to be organised, everything seemed to be rushed and all over the place. My dress was horrible, I had no shoes on and I even forgot to tell my dad about the wedding. I was crying my heart out so much saying I was about to make the worst mistake ever. I cried to my brother, he told me he knows but I shouldn't worry because everything will work out. There were so many people there but I did not want to tell everyone to leave to save the embarrassment and disgrace. It felt like the most horrific day of my life.

This was a dream I had 4 days after I finished university. I'm sure I got you thinking there for a minute.

After finishing university, there was a very valuable lesson God taught me, and He taught me that lesson through this dream. I did not take this dream literal, in the sense that it was about my marriage per se, but I knew it was to do with the decisions I make in life. God wanted me to understand that I must listen and follow His voice and His directions only, and how people's opinions and suggestions should be secondary to His. He wanted to teach me that in **this season** of my life, if people were to give direction, it should only confirm the word He has given; how I should not rely too much on what people think or say as it may be the cause of my downfall. In the dream, everybody was saying this guy was the one when I knew he was not, yet I was still going through with the marriage with tears in my eyes. God knew after university there would come a time where people's voices would have the potential to be the loudest voice in my ear and so was preparing me for how I would need to tackle that.

"Block out every other voice that is in your ear, and listen carefully for Mine. Do not allow the words of other people to get to you too much or even dictate what you do. You move as I the Lord instructs. Wait patiently and take heed to My instructions. It will be worth the wait".

These were the words God spoke directly to me 5 days after I had that dream. God was teaching me how to be His sheep. A Purpose Driven Woman is a woman who is a sheep of God, not a sheep of people. After this, I sought to study what it actually meant to be a sheep of God. To walk with God, you must first learn to be His sheep, because a sheep is always walking with their shepherd.

~ The Sheep of His Pasture ~

Who/what is a sheep?

A sheep is an animal that has the tendency to follow others; the word sheep is used to reference people who are easily influenced or led. In this context, you are a sheep and God is your shepherd; He is the only one you should be easily influenced or led by. The parable in the book of Luke chapter 19:1-7 talks about a lost sheep and a shepherd leaving the other 99 sheep just to find the one lost sheep.

Jesus was in deep pursuit of you, and He still is. He sought to look for you and desires you to look for Him. He left the 99 sheep just to search for the one; you were that one. When you were in your sin, 'living your best life' and had no care in the world, He still risked leaving the other 99 just to add you to the fold. We were all in a place of being a lost sheep, but God never gave up on us. He searched earnestly, and by searching earnestly for us, it shows He realises the need for a Saviour for the one lost sheep. Then by adding them to the fold, He realises their need for a shepherd to guide them, protect them and direct them.

A lot of us have realised our need for a saviour by accepting Jesus Christ into our lives, but have neglected the need for a shepherd now that we are in the fold. We want to take control and take charge of our own lives even though we are in the fold. We want to be acting like goats in a fold of sheep, but it does not work like that. Once we are in the fold, we are to comply with the ways of the fold; which is to possess the characteristics of a sheep, recognise and acknowledge our need for a shepherd, and sacrifice our will to follow our shepherd.

God is very intentional in using sheep as a metaphor for His children. Goats and sheep are very much similar in appearance but are completely different in character. Goats are independent, opinionated, vulgar, dangerous and destructive. Whereas sheep are dependent, harmless, they are defenceless without their shepherd and are protected from their environment (while the environment is protected from goats). It is so important we are able to identify with the characteristics of a sheep and not that of a goat.

Many of us are seeking direction and clarity from God concerning certain things, especially the discovery of this journey to fulfilling purpose, yet we are not His sheep. We recite *"The Lord is my Shepherd"* from Psalm 23, but know nothing about what it means to actually be His sheep! We live our lives independent of God and expect Him to have His way in our lives. How can He have His way if you think you know it all and think you have it all together? Anything God instructs you to do, you think your opinion matters above all and so do what *you* think is best or comfortable for you, rather than being obedient to your shepherd. You give the impression you are a sheep by outwardly complying to the ways of the fold, but inwardly you are vulgar, destructive and dangerous. Let's check ourselves. Let's stop deceiving ourselves, and begin behaving like the sheep of God. There will come a time where God will make a distinction between the two (Matthew 25:32-33), He will place His sheep at His right hand and the goats on His left, and believe me, you do not want to find yourself on the left.

Let's look at the characteristics of a sheep and see how we can begin possessing all of these characteristics. A sheep *follows* their shepherd because they are *dependent* on Him, not dependent on themselves, other people or their circumstances. Wherever you see a shepherd, the sheep are not too far behind following. When all hell is breaking loose, and nothing seems to be working out, a sheep of God does not take matters into their own hands, they continue to depend on their shepherd to come through for them; regardless of how tough or challenging the situation may be. Therefore, the question I ask you is: where do you find yourself? In front leading, trying to be the shepherd of your own life, or behind following? Do you make decisions and then consult God afterwards, or do you consult God before making certain life decisions? Some of us are 50% sheep and 50% goats; we want to do what pleases us, what is convenient for us, what is comfortable for us, and *still* ask God to lead us. That is error. A sheep who does not follow their shepherd *completely* is like a sheep without a shepherd, and a sheep without a shepherd is a lost and confused sheep. Some of us are lost and confused not because we don't have a shepherd or because the shepherd is not leading us, but because we just refuse to be obedient and follow Him. This goes to show that you can be in the fold and STILL be lost and confused; which is why we have many believers of Jesus Christ, but yet have no sense of direction in life. Now is the time to realign our focus, fix our eyes on Jesus and dedicate our lives to following Him. Direction is only given to those who are willing to follow. It is only a heart that is fully surrendered to God that will walk in obedience. Therefore, if obedience is something you struggle with, you must ask yourself whether your heart is fully surrendered to your Shepherd. We cannot be stubborn sheep.

Sheep are *specific* with what they *eat*, whereas goats feed on anything they find. Real life sheep's feed on grass because they know grass is the kind of food that is beneficial for them. As a sheep of God, what do you feed on?

Spiritually, what are you feeding yourself? What are you allowing to enter your eyes, your ears and eventually your heart? It is not anything and everything you find that you must eat. Not everything that you set your eyes on should be given access to your heart. Proverbs 4:23 tells us to guard our heart with all diligence because whatever is allowed into your heart is what will flow out of you. You can identify the kind of person somebody is simply by what they give out; in their speech and conduct. You must be specific with what you spend your time reading, with what you spend your time watching, with what you spend your time listening to! Why? Because you become what you read, you become what you watch, you become what you listen to, you become the conversations you entertain. If it does not contribute to your growth and development, get rid of it! As believers, we must get to a point where we are unapologetic about what we allow in our environment, simply because we understand the impact and effect it can have on us spiritually, physically and emotionally. Shepherds protect their sheep from their environment simply because the goats have contaminated the environment. Whether you believe it or not, everything you allow to enter you has an effect on you either positively or negatively.

GOD SAYS: "WALK WITH ME..."

There was a point in my life where all I listened to was Afrobeats; it made me happy! It made me happy but did not give me any satisfaction; learn to know the difference. Constantly listening to those songs fuelled my desire to attend events where the Spirit of God was nowhere to be found; being in such environments was so polluting to my spirit. I was just feeding my spirit with garbage. Not only was there ungodly music being played, but ungodly, immoral dances and ungodly beverages being consumed, which I eventually got myself involved in. So you see how one thing led to another, and then to another, simply because I was not specific with what I was feeding on.

As a sheep of God, feed on the right things and be unapologetic about feeding on the right things. Don't allow others to make you feel as though you are "too spiritual" simply because you have standards. It is only people who are not spiritual that will criticise other people for being spiritual. We are spiritual beings, we live by the Spirit, and so everything we do must be by the Spirit.

Even with things that give the impression to have the appearance of God, be specific! It is not every woman of God and it is not every man of God you must eat from. It is not every table you must accept the invitation to sit at. In these last days, the devil is getting more creative and using his agents to disguise themselves as angels of light. The bible talks about being aware of wolves in sheep's clothing (Matthew 7:15); in this perspective, I will make it 'goats in sheep's clothing'. There will be some sheep in the fold who will give the appearance of being a sheep but are in fact goats and wolves. As a sheep in the fold, you must also be discerning and alert. Yes, you are in the fold to follow your Shepherd and His directions, but do not follow blindly. Follow with discernment. Along the way, along the journey, other 'sheep' will enter the fold and it is important to realise that not everyone who enters will be genuine and true (John 10:1). They may have the skin of a sheep but the heart of a wolf and a goat; they may have the appearance of light, but will be full of utter darkness. It is not every sheep you must get close to and walk with; be discerning. They may prophesy, they may heal, they may speak in tongues, but the word of God tells us to test every spirit to see whether it is truly from God. Does everything about their lifestyle scream JESUS, or are there certain things that are questionable or contradict the word of God. Follow with discernment!

In order to discern fake from real, you must know the real, you must know the original. You cannot expect to determine whether somebody is true or counterfeit if you yourself aren't familiar with the truth.

GOD SAYS: "WALK WITH ME…"

A note to sheep: do not deceive yourself into thinking you are a sheep when really and truly you are a goat. Heart checks are so important; regularly examine and self-assess your heart to see if there are any traits of a goat. It is one thing to deceive others, but even worse to deceive yourself without even realising. Carry out a spiritual detox; ask the Lord to point out to you anything that may resemble a goat and ask Him to cleanse and purify your heart of anything that may not resemble a sheep.

A sheep of God *lives* and *walks by faith*, not sight. Literally. After finishing university, I wasn't sure whether God was leading me to pursue a Master's degree or just go straight into work, and so was very lost. As a sheep of God, you won't *always* know or be one hundred percent certain of where exactly God is leading or taking you, but you must do well to follow His directions. It is following His directions that require faith. Following a direction requires you to move, and making a move requires you to take a step or steps, and the steps you take will be leading you to the destination God is taking you. Even though you may not necessarily see the destination from the very beginning; though certain things along the way may cause you to think, doubt or question; though the instructions may not even make sense! But with every step you take, you must have faith to believe He is indeed leading you to the right place (Hebrews 11:1). Though you cannot see, you must believe. Sheep have poor eyesight, but when their shepherd calls them by name, they are able to recognise their voice and make their way towards their shepherd. They are able to find their shepherd according to the direction of where the voice came from. They follow the voice though they cannot see! To find their shepherd.

I was always a person who wanted to receive confirmation from people. I was never fully confident in the truth that God actually spoke to me, gave me directions and more; I always wanted somebody to be able to confirm what I already knew. I thought if somebody else was able to confirm, then indeed I heard correctly what God had said. But God needs us to be confident in what He says, regardless of whether other people are able to catch the vision or not. It is not all the time others will be able to see what you are seeing or hear what you are hearing. In times such as those, will you still believe or will you reject what God has said? You will be held accountable. A sheep of God is confident in the direction they personally receive from their shepherd. A sheep walks by faith, follows their shepherd by faith and reaches their destination by faith.

GOD SAYS: "WALK WITH ME…"

A sheep *stays* in the *presence* of *their shepherd*. Just as a shepherd knows their sheep, God knows you and I. However, John 10:14 (NKJV) says *"I know my own sheep, AND THEY ALSO KNOW ME"*.

Do we? It's a question.

God wants us to not *just* be acquainted with him, but to be **closely** and **intimately** acquainted with Him; in order to know and recognise His presence in our lives; to be aware of His promptings and direction; to know and be sensitive to all His sounds and noises; to know His heart and mind. When a sheep is newly added to the fold, it is not guaranteed they will be able to discern the ways, directions, promptings or voice of his shepherd from the very beginning; but the shepherd will know him because he is the one who adopted him into the fold. Nevertheless, as time goes on, the sheep would have been under the supervision and shepherding of his shepherd so much that he will begin to become acquainted with his shepherd. He would have been under the leadership and presence of the shepherd for so long that recognising the voice and presence of the shepherd will not be a problem anymore.

~ Staying in the presence
brings familiarity of the presence ~

John 10:27 (NKJV) – *"My sheep hear My voice, I know them and they follow Me."*

Your ability to hear and follow the voice of your Shepherd is dependent on how much you are acquainted with your Shepherd. How easy is it for you to distinguish the voice of your Shepherd from the voice of a stranger? Jesus said *"the voice of a stranger, they will not follow"* (John 10:3-5), because they **know** and can **identify** the voice of their Shepherd. It is time for the mediocre relationship with God to come to an end. The level God desires us to know Him is the same level Christ knows the Father (John 10:14-15); that is deep. We must go deeper. We must become more intimate, and intimacy with God requires effort and sacrifice. Christ sacrificed His life, what are you sacrificing? A sheep sacrifices their own will by staying in the presence of their Shepherd and following their shepherd. Your life is no longer your own (Galatians 2:20 & Romans 12:1).

~ "Walk with Me as Moses Walked with Me" ~

"Learn to walk with Me as Moses walked with Me" was an instruction I received from God. As a result, I studied how Moses walked with God. Moses was a man who as well as knowing the ways of God, knew the heart and mind of God. Moses was a man who spoke to God face to face as a man speaks to a friend; that is intimacy. Moses was Israel's access code to God; anytime Moses would meet God, whether in the Tabernacle or on the mountain, he would always come back with a word from God for the people. As a result, the people were dependent on Moses to hear what God had to say to them.

What God made me understand from this was that the behaviour of the children of Israel reflects the immaturity of the church today. We are too lazy to seek a personal and intimate relationship with God for ourselves; we want to be spoon fed like the children of Israel. Hence, what God wants us to understand is this: *"do not always desire to be spoon fed with revelations, prophecies, and knowledge. When you see people who are operating at that level of intimacy with Me, let it challenge you to reach there as well. There is nothing wrong with sitting at their feet to attain wisdom and knowledge, but do not let it be your only source of spiritual income."* We all have the capacity to become intimate with God.

From the many things I learnt from studying Moses, one major thing I took from him was how much he cherished the presence of God, and desired to do nothing and go nowhere without it. The same way a sheep stays in the presence of their Shepherd, staying in the presence of God must become an addiction and obsession for us. In Exodus chapter 33, it is recorded that God promised Moses to send an Angel before them to the land which He swore to give them; seeing as He refused to go with the people due to their stubbornness.

However, Moses was not satisfied with that condition; he wanted God Himself to go with them. He understood it was the presence of God that made all the difference. He understood it was the presence of God that would set them apart and distinguish them from all other people. In order to walk with God, you must cherish and desire His presence at all times; you must eat His presence, drink His presence, breathe His presence, abide in His presence.

To walk with God means to acknowledge His presence every hour, every minute, every second of the day. It means to be in continual fellowship, continual communion and 24-hour solitude with God. We are all aware that as believers, we **must** spend time with God through the reading, studying and the meditation of His word, through worship, praise and prayer. Whether we choose to do so in the morning, afternoon, evening or night. Yes, we cannot neglect that, but walking with God goes further than just 'spending time with God'. Noah and Enoch were both men who walked with God; they didn't *only* set apart specific times during the day to spend time with God, but they were also in communion with God even whilst they were doing everything else.

God seeks your attention constantly, God seeks you to abide in His presence consistently, not only when you spend dedicated time in devotion. When you are making your way to school, work or church, He wants you to commune with Him. When you are cooking and preparing a meal, He wants you to fellowship and commune with Him. Whatever activity you may be engaging in during the day, He wants you to fellowship and commune with Him. Do not only engage with God during devotion time, and neglect Him during the many remaining hours of the day. It is imperative we ask God to allow our spirit to continually be in tune with Him and make us more sensitive and alert to His presence daily. God is always communicating with us but sometimes we fail to grasp what He is trying to communicate because we are not *consistently* in tune.

When you walk with someone, you begin to learn more about their ways, their character, and their preferences. If you have a friend you've been walking with for years, you will know it is true. God made Himself known to Moses personally in Exodus chapter 34 by proclaiming His name to him. If anyone was to ask Moses who God was, he now had a perfect answer because he had received a personal revelation of God's name and nature. *Desire to have a personal revelation of God for yourself*.

This personal revelation, I believe, was as a result of Moses asking God to see His glory in the previous chapter. When Moses asked God to see His glory, God made him understand that no one would be able to see Him and survive, so He showed Moses His back and hand. However, the lesson to be learnt here is that Moses is the one who initiated this level of intimacy; he took the first step. God did not just decide to show him His back and hand, it was all because Moses asked to see. If we desire to go deeper in our intimacy with God, we must be the ones to initiate it. If we desire to walk with God and become a friend of God, we must purpose in our hearts to do so. We must be the ones who desire and make an effort to go deeper. God did not force His glory on Moses, Moses asked for it! God will never withhold Himself from us; He desires us more than we desire Him. If we ask for more of Him, He will not hesitate to give us more. Psalm 42:7 (NKJV) – "*deep calls unto deep…*" the deep things of God are revealed unto those who go deep. There is always more of God to desire; don't be satisfied with what you already know or with what you have already seen. Yearn for more.

Before God gave Moses a personal revelation of His name in chapter 34, God brought him up to the mountain *by himself.* God will first need to bring you to a place of solitude before handing out revealed truths and insights. Moses was in this place of solitude for 40 days and nights without food or drink and did not complain; but when it is time for us to spend even 1 hour in solitude with God, we get tired and restless. Being in a place of solitude is a 24-hour thing. Your mind and spirit must always be in a state whereby it is at liberty and is one with God, and alone with God.

> ❖ *Solitude = the state of being alone without necessarily feeling lonely; a state of peace and quiet.*

When you are always in this state, you are then *always* in the position to receive from God. Walking with God requires 24-hour solitude, both consciously or subconsciously.

Once God told Moses to come up to the mountain in the morning, He told him to 'present' himself to Him there. The word 'present' in Hebrew means 'to stand upright, take an upright position, to be in your best state'. In other words, God was saying *"do not come up to Me on the mountain anyhow; you must be prepared and stationed appropriately when you come into My presence. Let your mind, spirit and your body be positioned correctly"*. This is why when it comes to spending dedicated intimate time with God, as well as walking with Him throughout your day, it cannot be effective if you are half awake or if your mind is consumed with many thoughts and worries. God simply wants all your attention, but that cannot happen if we are not wide awake at the time we are having devotion or if our mind is already occupied.

How do we expect God to minister to us if we are in and out of prayer because we are in and out of sleep?

God wants *all* of you to Himself, He doesn't want divided attention because a mind that is divided cannot comprehend fully the mysteries and insights of God. God is jealous for you (2 Corinthians 11:2) and your attention; if we are constantly giving our attention to sleep, our phones or our many thoughts, He becomes jealous. God is like a husband who yearns and longs for his wife's attention. If a husband sees his wife giving her attention to something else at the time he is supposed to be having it, the husband will ultimately become jealous. It is the same with God; we are His bride and He is our bridegroom. A bride who is seen to be giving her attention and love to other things or people even before the wedding will be characterised as being unfaithful, therefore, how much more after the wedding. God told Moses to let no one come up to the mountain with him, and that no one should even be seen throughout the mountain; this is how much God wanted Moses all to Himself. God is calling you all to Himself, will you go?

    Sometimes, one way God will enjoy having you all to Himself is by literally being still before Him. There will be times where I can feel a pulling or a tugging on my heart to literally just sit at the feet of God in quietness. It's what you call the prayer of "inner quietness". I would play a soft instrumental in the background and just sit or lie down in silence and say "God, I'm all yours". It is literally just enjoying the stillness of His presence without any distractions. Many of us are prayer warriors, we shout and we scream, but we lack a sense of stillness and intimacy in our prayer life. Yes, there is a time to scream and shout, but we must also learn when and how to be still; to encounter God every day and enjoy His presence, we must understand the prayer of inner quietness. "To sink down into the depths of Christ and become comfortable in that posture". Pause for a moment and silently think about this God you love; Whose power is beyond all. In this moment is when you hear the still quiet voice of God, or when you can literally feel His overwhelming presence. Sometimes, that is all He desires from us. As much as we should desire His presence, we should know that He also desires ours.

> *"Coming before God in quietness, and waiting upon Him in silence can accomplish more than many days of feverish activity."*
> *- A.W. Tozer*

Another way God may call you unto Himself is by separating you or "isolating" you from your friendships for a period of time. All of a sudden, you may see that your friends aren't communicating with you as frequently anymore or you personally begin to feel as though you have nobody around you to speak to. It's not loneliness, it's God calling you.

There were two instances in the book of Exodus whereby God brought Moses up to the mountain of Sinai. The first time Moses spent 40 days and nights on the mountain (Exodus 24), he had to wait and rest in the cloud of God's glory for 6 days before actually being called to the top of the mountain to be with God. This shows the process of intimacy with God. Biblically, the number 7 represents completion. For God to wait 6 days and call Moses up on the seventh day symbolises how Moses was being prepared by God before being able to ascend the mountain. Intimacy with God is a process; becoming intimate with someone happens over a period a time. This passage of scripture makes it clear that a face to face relationship with God does not happen overnight. God may take you through a season of seeking, pursuing and waiting to see how much you really desire the face to face, and intimate relationship. The 6 days here is symbolic of the waiting, seeking and pursuing; the seventh day is symbolic of the period whereby God sees you are ready to be taken to another level. The days in this sense are not literal but are symbolic and representative of process.

The second time Moses was called up to Mount Sinai in chapter 34, he goes straight to the top. Why? Intimacy has already been established; he did not need to wait another '6 days' to be called to the top because he is still at the level of intimacy God brought him to. People who are intimate with God do not struggle or have to work hard to continually be in the presence of God; just as an eagle does not struggle to fly because they have learnt to become more experienced in it.

Although intimacy is a process, you won't always realise the time God takes you to higher levels in your intimacy with Him. It won't be as evident as you think; what you must do is just endure and enjoy the process. When I look at my life and my intimacy with God, I can say I have indeed moved up in levels, but I did not necessarily take notice of it at the time. It is only now I can see a difference when I reminisce, and I know there are still higher levels to attain. Moses himself did not realise his face was shining with the glory of God after coming down from the mountain; it was the children of Israel who made it known to him. It is a popular fact that husbands and wives begin to look alike when they have become more intimate, have borne children and are continually in close proximity. They do not notice that they begin to look alike, but they do. It is the same with intimacy with God. Sometimes, you won't notice the changes; but be assured you are indeed making progress and intimacy is indeed being built. The process cannot be rushed; intimacy does not have shortcuts.

~ Seek God, Not the Assignment ~

There was a **very crucial** lesson God taught me in my quest to discovering and fulfilling purpose: Do not pursue the assignment more than you pursue God Himself!

I was guilty of falling into this trap. I wanted to know my purpose so much but yet forsook to know the God of my purpose! Even though Moses was on an assignment of leading a nation for God, God still brought Moses to Himself. You cannot be on a mission for God without even knowing God, and this is the mistake some of us make. We want to know our purpose, we want to know what God has called us to do, yet we do not even desire to know God Himself. God did not want Moses to fall into the danger doing that, and so brought him to a place of solitude for 40 days and nights, twice.

Even when you are on assignment for God, you must continually draw to Him and from Him, so that you do not lose yourself in the process. Even in the process of the assignment, you cannot always be out in the presence of the people; there will be times where you will need to draw away from the crowd and from the people intentionally and draw into God. I constantly had to remind myself as I was writing this book to not get carried away in the writing of this book and forget Him in the process; that I still need to draw into God and from Him. We must not seek the assignment more than we seek God Himself. Without God there would be no assignment in the first place. We do not only walk with God until the 'go ahead'. We should not only be faithful and consistent in the way we walk with God until that 'thing' comes. Whatever the 'thing' may be: marriage, a job, business, purpose. Do not forget it is by walking with Him that you reached that place, so you must continue with the same effort and desire in order to sustain and maintain the place you have reached. When God gives the go-ahead, He is not saying "go" or "it is time for *you* to go now". What He's saying is "Let *us* go" and "it is time for *us* to move now".

Even now, God is saying: *"ALWAYS walk with Me, even when I Am the One who sends you. Understand that when I send you, your assignment cannot be fully fulfilled unless I the Lord is with you"*.

We must get this right; do not neglect God in your pursuit to becoming a Purpose Driven Woman. Intimacy with God is not necessarily *what* you do for Him, but *who* you are to Him. God is not looking for the fulfilment of your purpose as a replacement of your devotion and intimacy. He is looking for you to be solely devoted to Him, and as a result of that, your service to Him will become influential and effective. Your service to Him will become effortless simply if you stay devoted to Him. Jesus Christ came on earth to do nothing else other than the will of His Father. As a result of devoting Himself to His Father, walking in the fulfilment of His purpose, people becoming saved, healed and delivered was the natural outcome. Your devotion to God must be the primary thing, in order to serve Him and fulfil purpose. In fact, your major service to Christ is your personal devotion to Him. Jesus asked Simon Peter three times whether he loved Him in John 21:15-17. Jesus wanted to make Peter understand that he could only take care of His sheep if he really loved Him; his service to Him could only work if he personally devoted himself to Him.

Don't have a desire for the cause, but not a desire for Reason for the cause. Don't have a desire for the hype but not a desire for the One you hype for. It's so easy to get lost in the hype of "service" and "purpose" that you forget the One whom you are serving and are on an assignment for. You can love your purpose and assignment so much without even loving Christ. Don't get confused and fall into that trap.

It was when I started to learn how to be a sheep of God and to walk with God that I began to realise walking in the fulfilment of your purpose will become effortless once you learn to walk with God. When you walk with somebody, it implies that you are in line with them. Walking with God keeps you in alignment with Him. When you walk with God every day, you are ultimately walking in purpose every day. As I mentioned, when I completed university, I was lost and confused in terms of what I had to do next. However, when I became intentional about keeping my eyes fixed on God by walking with Him, I eventually found myself writing this book as a result of simply following His directions; which *was* His plan and purpose. I had to keep my eyes fixed in order to know what to do next. Though I did not have a job, though I did not have a stable income, God gave me specific instructions: become My sheep and walk with Me. When nothing seemed to make sense, when nobody else understood, I was obedient and did as instructed. Then as a result of taking heed to these instructions, purpose was being fulfilled. Stay simply devoted & keep your eyes fixed on Jesus Christ.

God is saying "walk with Me…".

GOD SAYS: "WALK WITH ME…"

Prayer:

Most gracious and loving Father, it is my desire to become Your sheep. It is my desire to learn to walk with You. Therefore, I ask that You help and prune me into becoming the sheep of Your pasture; to possess the characteristics of a sheep and see You as my Good Shepherd. Lord, give me a desire for Your presence; to stay and abide in Your presence 24 hours a day. Continue to teach me what it means to walk with You in order to stay in line with You and Your purpose. I desire and long for You alone, above everything else. In the Name of Jesus Christ, Amen.

"She walked with God; that was her game changing strategy."

5

Embrace Every Season, Enjoy The Journey

Everybody goes through different seasons in their lives, whether positive or negative. However, these seasons we go through are all for a specific purpose. They make up for this lifetime journey we undergo in order to reach the destination God has purposed each of us to reach. Every season we find ourselves in teaches us something new, which causes growth. When we see ourselves growing, we see progress is being made. We cannot expect to see progress in our lives if we are not willing to take the necessary steps to grow.

If you find yourself in a particular season but you are not taking full advantage of that season, trying to see how it has the potential to develop you as a person, and yet still want to see progress, it's not going to happen. All these different seasons are lessons teaching and building you up to reach your final destination. It's all a process, preparing you for the greater things in store later in the next seasons. Think about it, you don't start at the top and work your way down, you start from the bottom and work your way up. There are certain seasons you may have previously found yourself in or find yourself in now, and you are thinking to yourself or asking God "when will this pass?".

You must make the most of every season you find yourself in; God is *always* teaching us and causing us to learn.

EMBRACE EVERY SEASON, ENJOY THE JOURNEY

Don't wish away the difficult seasons, because it is always in the difficult seasons that God does His most important work. One preacher said, *"the season that you wish away is most often the season that you learn the most from";* which is absolutely true. Embrace every season you find yourself in, try and figure out what exactly God wants you to learn from that particular season, and enjoy the journey.

Remember, purpose is a journey; not all journeys are smooth and direct. Sometimes there are humps, sometimes there are delays, sometimes there are transits, but be rest assured that you shall surely reach your final destination.

There was a period of time when I used to be so hooked onto the TV series 'Scandal' and 'The Haves and The Haves Nots'. I would stay up until 3 am, sometimes 4 am just watching episode after episode. Every last episode I watched would make me excited to watch the next one. The number of times I told myself "Okay, last one" but found myself watching another one was countless. I was so eager to know what was going to happen next. It was actually a very bad addiction, but *girlll* thank God I've been delivered now. In a reality TV show or any TV series, something new always happens in every episode, sometimes things you don't expect which catch you off guard; which is why we desire to know what is going to happen next. We go ahead of ourselves.

Sadly, we behave the same way with our life's purpose; we want to know everything that's going to happen next forgetting that journeys require time and patience.

What season do you currently find yourself in? Once you have identified it, do you see yourself trying to skip that season and enter into the next even though you have not fully fulfilled the purpose for your current season?

In school, you begin by starting off in reception, then you go to year 1, year 2, year 3 and so forth. Rarely do you ever see people jump years; only if their mental capacity has been proved to be beyond their age. Life is not a rush; nobody is in your lane with you, you are in your own lane, therefore stay in your own lane and allow God to take you through the different seasons of your life. Trust me, when it is time to enter into the next season, you will know.

So how do you identify the season you find yourself in? To be able to answer the question, you will first need to ask yourself these questions:

1. In what environment/s do I find myself in? (School, college, university, work, home, church?)
2. In the environment/s I find myself in, is there anything significant happening around me or to me? (a situation, a major life event, etc.)

3. If there *is* anything happening around me or to me, how am I feeling? What does God need me to learn or what would God want me to do in order to be influential and bring impact? (depending on what's happening around you, God may be teaching you how to exercise patience; He may need you to start a fellowship because there's a lot of immorality; He may need you to learn what it means to be organised, etc.)

When it comes to seasons, you will find yourself *doing* something that will ultimately be *teaching* you something. For instance, somebody may find themselves in a season of mentorship and pouring out; God will be teaching them what it means to be able to pour into the lives of others in that season because they find themselves mentoring so many people. Another person may find themselves in a season of crushing and stretching because they are being tried on every side at their work place. God will ultimately be teaching them what it means to be crushed and stretched, in a sense that they feel as though too much is being required of them in that season. The purpose of the crushing and stretching will be for them to know after the crushing, new wine will be produced. They would have been stretched to capacity so much they would now have the capability to do more than what was even required of them in their previous season. Appreciating the purpose of every season is so necessary.

When we look at the life of Moses again, we see how he fulfilled purpose in seasons. For some of us, the reason why we neglect fulfilling purpose in seasons is because we have seen the bigger picture. God has revealed to us we will preach to nations and preach boldly in the name of Jesus all around the world, or we have received prophetic words upon prophetic words telling us what God is going to do with our lives. Therefore, because of this, we feel as though we only need to wait until that time in order to "fulfil purpose", and not do anything now. We have come to understand that purpose is a journey which we grow and develop in, that when you walk with God every day, you are ultimately walking in purpose every day. Therefore, thinking you must only wait until the bigger picture is the wrong mentality to have.

The purpose God has assigned for you is not only limited to the bigger picture. Wherever you find yourself, do not think the purpose and mandate upon your life is "too great" and "powerful" to be manifested now. Putting to use and walking in the applicable knowledge and revelation of your purpose and mandate during each and every season of your life is how you grow and develop in purpose. Do not think the mandate is going to drop on top of your head one day and then you will all of a sudden begin to operate in the full power and authority of your purpose and mandate. If you know you have been called to preach to nations, preach to a small audience now; if you know you carry a great seed that has the potential to transform the world, allow that seed to transform your Jerusalem now; if you know you have been called to enter the entertainment industry, start making your own short films/series **now**.

Even though Moses had not yet been given the assignment of delivering and leading a nation, he still behaved and lived as what God destined and purposed him to be: a deliverer and a leader. He delivered the Hebrew slave from the hand of the Egyptian who was maltreating him and killed the Egyptian; he saved the seven daughters of Jethro and delivered them from the shepherds at the well in Midian; he was given a flock of sheep to tend and shepherd by his father in law; AND THEN he was given a NATION to deliver and lead from the land of Egypt. So yes, there may be a greater assignment/s in the latter seasons of your life, but you must give God a reason to trust you with the greater assignment; which is by proving yourself to be faithful with the little.

We must seek to be purposeful and influential in our immediate surroundings during every season of our lives before desiring to be purposeful and influential in our nation. It starts where you are and where you have been placed now.

When Jesus Christ told the disciples to go and make disciples of all nations, He indirectly told them to start with their immediate surroundings, which was Jerusalem; and then they should go to Judea, Samaria, and the uttermost parts of the earth. To be very honest, as much as we seek to be purposeful and influential in our immediate surroundings, we will indirectly be having an influence on our nation, simply because our nation is made up of our immediate surroundings. Wherever you find yourself now, in school, at university, your workplace, your business, your church; seek to have an impact there now!

When I went to university, I was told: "God did not send you to university *only* to get a degree, there is a greater purpose". By the time I knew it, I was leading a campus fellowship at my university, teaching the word of God and leading discussions every week to a group of people. That season of my life was a very stretching season for me; I didn't like public speaking but I had to understand it was preparation for what is yet come and so embrace the season.

However, please understand, having an impact in your immediate surroundings is not only limited to standing on a stage, holding a mic or being on a pulpit. God does not just call us to places of influence in the church or church settings but also outside the church. You won't spend your entire life within the four walls of the church building; you will ultimately find yourself beyond the four walls, and when you do, be impactful and influential.

In your conversations with people, let it be impactful; let your words be seasoned with grace, counsel, and wisdom. In the way you help others, let it be impactful. Even in your conduct, the way you portray yourself, let it be impactful. If you work with children and students, preach the bible to them without necessarily quoting scripture; encourage them by letting them know they can do all things, let them know the sky is not their limit and that they can achieve whatever they put their minds to. It is very possible to have an impact in every environment you find yourself in regardless of what season you do find yourself in.

Another thing to understand is if you find yourself in a particular season, don't think you cannot help or support somebody else who may be in the same season. It is possible for God to be teaching you both different things that may be of benefit to each of you. I remember when I was in my season of emotional healing, I was mentoring a girl who also needed emotional healing. I thought to myself, "how can I be mentoring somebody who is going through the exact same thing as me"? But as a result, even as I was mentoring her, God was teaching me more than I believe I would have learnt if I wasn't mentoring and guiding her through her own emotional healing journey.

~ Understand Your Own Times and Seasons ~

Seasons can vary. You can find yourself in "a season of" anything and everything; a season of healing, a season of working, a season of serving, a season of rest, a season of being broken, a season of financial increase, a season of deliverance, a season of sowing, a season of harvesting, a season of learning, a season of birthing, and a lot more. It is all about what God is trying to make you **prioritise** in those seasons. You won't be able to prioritise *everything* at the same time in life, which is why you must learn to understand your *own* times and seasons, to know what God is requiring of you in those specific times. When you understand your own times and seasons, you won't measure your progress, your achievements or your journey against others; you won't do things prematurely, nor will you allow what God is asking of you to be far overdue. When I finally understood it wasn't my season of working, when people would approach me and ask me about my job search, it got to a point where it didn't pressurise me or cause me to think I need to catch up. Solely because I knew it wasn't *my* season to be prioritising full-time work.

Understanding your own times and seasons will save you from deviating from purpose because you begin to understand what *you* need to do. In John 6:15, the bible states that Jesus perceived the people were coming to take Him and make Him a king by force. When He realised what they wanted to do, He departed to the mountain by Himself alone. The people were trying to make Jesus enter His season of manifestation and glory, though it was not yet time. Jesus understood His own times and seasons and understood it was not yet time for His season of manifestation. Just because the people around you are saying "start the business, start the ministry, write the book" does not always mean it is a sign or confirmation for you to start *now*. This is where a lot of us make mistakes. We are more in tune with people than we are with God, so we lose focus, or worse yet, have no knowledge at all of what He is telling us to do.

YOU must understand *what* is being required of you and *when* it is required of you. Otherwise, the early entering of specific seasons will have the potential to destroy you; simply because you did the right thing but at the wrong time. The only person you should be seeking your confirmation and validation from is God. Jesus knew it was not yet His time to be glorified and so went back into a place of solitude and consecration. You cannot be consecrated for the people if you are not first consecrated to God.

There are numerous amount of times when Jesus said: "my hour has not yet come". Jesus knew the importance of doing things at the *right* and *appointed* time; and as well as knowing the importance, He knew WHEN it was the right and appointed time to do certain things. We must live our lives like this. We need to know when exactly we must do the things that are required of us. We need to know the prime time of our lives. This can only happen when we allow ourselves to continually be in tune with God and allow Him to lead us season by season.

Let's briefly look at the story of Esther. When Esther entered the king's palace, I'm sure she didn't know she was going to find favour in the eyes of Hegai; when she found favour with Hegai, I'm sure she didn't know she would be chosen as queen. When she was chosen as queen, I'm sure she didn't know a time would come whereby she would need to deliver her people from the hand of Haman. This was all purpose at work, but in seasons. She embraced every season. There is always a reason for the positions you find yourself in. The position you are in right now, do not overlook it; you have been placed there for a purpose and for this season particularly. Embrace it and do not take it for granted. You are there to do something, to make a change, to bring about a difference, to leave a mark and to leave a legacy. When you learn to embrace every season, you begin to realise that what God made you prioritise in your current season was necessary for your next season. Embrace every season, and enjoy the journey, purpose is being fulfilled.

Prayer:

Abba, help me to embrace every season of my life I find myself in. Help me to understand and appreciate the purpose in every season; help me to grasp everything You are and will be trying to teach me in this season now and the seasons to come. I pray for the ability to understand and discern my OWN times and seasons, as well as what You require of me and when. I also pray for the grace and confidence to embrace every season and enjoy the journey. In the mighty Name of Jesus Christ I pray, Amen.

"I rarely know where I am going in my life's journey, but I look back and see that God has been leading my every step and I did not even know it."

- A.W. Tozer

6

Set Boundaries,

Have Standards

As a believer of Jesus Christ, boundaries are necessary and standards are necessary. A believer without boundaries and standards is a person who will allow and accept anything and everything; which isn't an ideal way to live. A PDW sets standards and boundaries for herself.

Boundaries = *the limit of a subject or principle*. Boundaries are set to increase self-control; boundaries are set so they are not crossed; boundaries are set to develop discipline; boundaries are set to increase your credibility and integrity.

Standards = *a moral rule that should be obeyed*. Standards are set so that you do not settle for less; standards must be reached; standards must be kept and respected regardless of your circumstance.

Everybody will have different boundaries and standards, and they will be subjective to their purpose and what God has called them to do. That is why you cannot judge or criticise somebody for having specific standards and boundaries. Not everybody is the same and not everybody has the same purpose in life; the standards and boundaries used to govern your life should be steering you towards the direction of your purpose in every way. Even with children; clear guidance must be given specifically from God in order

SET BOUNDARIES, HAVE STANDARDS

to train them up in the way that they should go. The standards and boundaries that are set for a child must be in alignment with their purpose. You cannot raise each child in a family the same way, because they do not have the same future.

Clear instructions were given to Samson's parents in the way they should raise him simply because of the call and assignment God had placed upon his life. It was specific to the God-ordained purpose. Samson's parents asked the Angel of the Lord for direction in how to raise their son (Judges 13:12); that is what you call purposeful parenting. His parents were told a razor should never touch his head because he would be dedicated as a Nazarite to God. Nazarite's were Israelites who were set apart for the service of God and were obliged to abstain from alcohol, never cut their hair and never have contact with dead bodies (Numbers 6:1-8). These were the boundaries and standards that were given to Samson; they were not given to him to restrict him, but simply because of purpose! There are certain things God will make us understand we need to refrain from just because we need to fulfil purpose.

What boundaries and standards is God directing you to set in your life? Are you adhering and respecting those boundaries? Nobody will respect your boundaries and standards if you do not respect them yourself. In your friendships, what are your standards and boundaries? In your family relations, what are your standards and boundaries? Even in your own life, what standards and boundaries have you set for yourself?

Boundaries and standards must be set in everything: what you watch, what you listen to, where you go (as we spoke about in chapter 4), your friendships, your relationship with God, your appearance, your lifestyle habits, eating habits, your health, and your conversations. Train yourself to cut off conversations that lead to useless talk, gossip, and slander. Be unapologetic about cutting off conversations that you notice have the potential to turn into gossip the minute you see it diverting. The antidote to avoiding godless speech is to *cultivate* godliness in your speech. Cultivating and promoting godliness reduces godless behaviour. As Purpose Driven Women, we must ensure that the words of our mouth are acceptable in the eyes of God.

Here are a few examples of boundaries I set for myself some time ago: not being on social media past 11pm, except in exceptional circumstances (it was a very hard boundary not to cross as you can imagine); not spending over the monthly limit of money I set myself; and not going above and beyond for a guy who has not made clear intentions. Examples of standards I set for myself were: all my relationships must be purposeful and intentional; to not settle for a guy whose purpose is not in line with my own; and that God remains no.1 in all things. There are a lot more boundaries and standards I have set for myself, but these are the few I shared to make clear the difference between the two.

Do not set boundaries and standards just for the sake of setting them; they must be dependent on you as a person, where God is taking you and what He needs you to do. They can be set based on what you need discipline for, habits you believe you need to start developing or levels you believe you need to reach. The reason why I set the boundary of not being on social media past 11pm was because I needed to practice and improve the art of being disciplined and reduce the amount of time I spend on social media. I noticed the amount of time I spent on social media was ridiculous and so took the necessary actions to tackle that. If you don't know how to be disciplined with your time, the enemy will do all he can to steal your time. Time is something you cannot get back; if we do not use our time wisely, procrastination will find its place. Procrastination delays purpose.

When it came to my friendships, I set the standard of prioritising purposeful and intentional relationships because I realised the destination which God is taking me, it is imperative I associate myself with people who are serious and radical about their walk with God. You become like the people you walk with. If you walk with people who have vision, you will also have vision. If you walk with people who are wise, you will also become wise. With the standards and the boundaries that you set, you must have sensible reasons as to why you set them, as well as the outcome you wish to see as a result of setting them.

As a Purpose Driven Woman, one area where we must be intentional and purposeful about setting standards is the way we dress! 1 Timothy 2:9 tells women to be modest in their appearance, as well as to wear decent and appropriate clothing. Clothing is a very controversial topic when it comes to Christian women. Some say it is down to personal conviction, others say it is dependent on the body shape of the woman, and a lot more. However, the fundamental factor to recognise is that as a woman of Christ and in Christ, our dressing is a form of worship God expects from us. When we render the fruit of our lips as a form of worship to our Maker, we are intentional about the words we utter. We never find ourselves uttering words that are not characteristic of God. We tell Him Who He is, we describe who He is and beautify Him with our words. In the same manner, our appearance should be intentional about describing God, beautifying Him and giving Him recognition. Your appearance should set you apart and allow others to see the God in you, not give them a distorted view of God. We must ask ourselves whether our dressing is indeed the kind of worship God will find acceptable. Your dressing is a form of worship EVERYWHERE you go, not just in church or at Christian events. As a woman in Christ, if you have categories of clothes (e.g. Church clothing, dinner/birthday clothing, holiday clothing) because you feel as though your dinner and holiday clothing cannot be worn to church because of its inappropriateness, then there is a problem. If it is inappropriate to wear to church, then it is inappropriate to wear anywhere. Everything you wear should be appropriate to wear anywhere. There is nothing wrong with having a category of clothes for the right reasons, but the reason for having the categories should not be because one category cannot be seen on you by your church members and the other can.

When it comes to our appearance, the Holy Spirit must have a say; as 'strange' as it may sound, it is the truth. Why do we allow the Holy Spirit to guide certain aspects of our lives but not others? The Holy Spirit is our guide for every single thing, especially when it comes to our appearance. Firstly, because we are representatives of Christ, we must be representing Him appropriately in every way.

Secondly, we should not find ourselves to be accountable for the 'falling' of our fellow brothers. I understand it is not always our fault if guys lustfully fall after us, but in the best way we know how to, let us ensure we are doing *all* we can to remain **blameless** when it comes to our appearance. We do that by allowing the Holy Spirit to guide our decisions and preferences when it comes to dressing. We must protect our dignity! Sisters, we shouldn't feel okay showcasing ourselves in an immodest manner! A Purpose Driven Woman clothes herself with dignity; she is a woman who understands that how she clothes herself is what qualifies her to be called a woman of virtue and purpose. Therefore, we must be purposeful even in our appearance! Father, we pray that our dressing as Purpose Driven Women will be an acceptable form of worship in your sight. Amen.

One thing that can sometimes stand in the way of us setting boundaries and standards is our fleshly emotions. We allow ourselves to be led by our emotions instead of being disciplined in doing what we know we need to do. I've been torn between the two on numerous occasions; where I've either had the choice of being straight and plain with someone or allowing my emotions to control me so the emotions of the other person would be spared. However, being a slave to my emotions has caused me to end up in situations I found very hard to come out of; which is so dangerous and draining! There was a time where I was entertaining the attention, compliments, and friendliness of a guy; there were times where this guy would literally cross boundaries in the things he would say to me, and I knew I had to let him know where the line should not be crossed. Due to my lack of discipline in setting boundaries, I actually found myself in an "indirect relationship". Although he made intentions clear, I had not said anything, so there was no agreement to anything. Yet, because my actions and responses did not condemn his doings, I caused the situation to become worse; just because I did not want to 'hurt his feelings'. Our fleshly emotions will lead us to places God never intended us in going because as believers, we are to be led by the Holy Spirit, not our emotions. Fleshly emotions are only temporary feelings that come based on a certain issue or situation we have faced; they do not stay or last. We experience different types of emotions all the time, so making decisions or taking actions based on this temporary emotion will only cause us to regret later on. That is why even our emotions must be surrendered to the Holy Spirit. A simple prayer such as "Holy Spirit, arrest my emotions" can save us from a lot of unnecessary havoc. We must choose to set boundaries over being slaves to our emotions.

For some of us, if we do not set boundaries, we will deviate from purpose. If boundaries are not set, purpose will be aborted! If you need to stop receiving phone calls at a certain time, stop receiving them! If you need to limit the conversations you have with certain people, limit them! If you need to dismantle that relationship, dismantle it! We **must** discipline ourselves. Without discipline, we will never reach the place God wants us to reach. It's about time we prioritise our purpose above what we desire "in the moment". One moment without discipline has the potential to defer a whole assignment.

I always thought setting clear boundaries and standards for your life would cause you to come across as rude or too "holier than thou", because that is honestly how some people would make you feel. So ultimately, you would refrain from doing so just to spare the opinions and criticisms of other people. Nonetheless, it does get to a point whereby the decisions you make in life, and the standards and boundaries you set in life, must not be dependent on the immaturity of others or their inability to accept your decisions, but on the leading and direction of God. As mentioned previously, not everybody will understand the standards and boundaries you set for yourself; but that must not stop you from living an intentional life.

SET BOUNDARIES, HAVE STANDARDS

Proverbs 27:5 NLT– *"an open rebuke is better than hidden love"*. In this context, an open rebuke would be the setting of standards and boundaries (because many people will ultimately be offended by the standards you set), and the hidden love representative of you constantly trying to spare the emotions of others instead of making it clear to the person what is acceptable and what is not. Sometimes, rebuke is needed, sometimes the truth needs to be told, sometimes people's immaturity needs to be confronted; all in a loving and Christ-like manner.

Jesus Christ Himself was accused of being a demon because He spoke the truth (John 8:48). The truth he spoke was hard for the people to understand so they resulted in accusing Him of being a demon. Jesus Christ, the Son of God, accused of being a demon; just thinking about it is funny. Not everybody will understand you because not everybody will be able to go in the direction you are going. We should not get upset when we are not compatible with certain people anymore. When it comes to all types of relationships, even your family, it is inevitable that a time will come whereby people will misunderstand you. But even when people do misunderstand you, do not lower your standards.

Friendships are one the hardest relationships to set boundaries and standards in because everybody wants to be friends forever. However, you won't be well-suited with everybody forever. You may still be friends, but just not as close as you used to be. There will come a time where you will begin to find yourself developing covenant friendships with people; whereby everything in that friendship is driven by purpose and your determination to fulfil purpose in each other's lives. You won't be in covenant friendships with everyone purely because not everyone is connected to your purpose. Many of us will have general types of friendships; friends whom we are associated with because of school, work, church or other connections. However, covenant friendships are friendships specifically driven by purpose. Do not desire to be in a covenant friendship with somebody if you are not going to serve any purpose in their lives and if you are not going to be an influential factor in helping them to fulfil purpose.

The ability to make a distinction between covenant friendships and general friendships is needed, simply because people serve different purposes in our lives. We must know the specific purpose certain people are to fulfil in our lives so that we do not entrust into their hands the wrong things. Jesus Christ was specific and made distinctions when it came to His relationships. There were times you would see Him with the multitude, times where He would be with the

12, times where He would be with the 3 and He also had the one whom the bible records as the one "He loved". When Jesus went up to the Mount of Transfiguration, it was only Peter, James and John whom He took with Him. Therefore, even Jesus understood it is not everybody whom you would need to walk with all the time. He was purposeful in whom He allowed to see that moment of glory and transparency on the mount.

Who you are associated with matters; you must be walking with people who have vision. Moses' mother saw a deliverer in her son before he even became a deliverer. Moses had just been born, it was not in his power or ability to see the potential in his life and so save his life. Therefore, it was important his mother was able to see beyond the physical. Sometimes all it takes is for someone to see and reveal the potential in you in order for purpose and destiny to be birthed. Be associated with the right people! Moses was surrounded by people who saw from the very day he was born, hence why he was catapulted into purpose and destiny just 3 months after his birth. Three months later, he found himself in pharaoh's palace, in the arms of pharaoh's daughter. That is the power of association. Being surrounded by people who can see spiritually and prophetically catapults you into divine destiny.

Set boundaries with your friends, let them know when it's time to play and when it's time to be serious. Let them know it is not every day that you are available. Let them know your relationship with Christ comes first before anything. Let them know they shouldn't speak into your life anyhow. Let them know that it is not everything about you they must know. Here a few questions to ask yourself in order to know whether your friendships are purposeful or purposeless:

1. What is the foundation of that friendship?
2. Are you drawing closer to discovering/fulfilling purpose in that friendship?
3. What is it in that friendship that you do the most?
4. Are you building each other up in faith?
5. Or bringing each other down in gossip?
6. What is it in that friendship that you have in common?
7. Are the commonalities purposeful or useless?
8. Are your conversations edifying or draining?
9. If you were to get rid of the main things you do or share in that friendship, would the friendship still be there?

Don't find yourself in an unnecessary friendship where there is no progress or uplifting, and where you aren't helping or building each other to grow and fulfil purpose.

SET BOUNDARIES, HAVE STANDARDS

Set boundaries with that guy who is trying to make his intentions known to you. Let him know that you have a standard. Let him know that you are a queen and precious in God's sight so you are to be treated as such. Let him know that you do not owe him anything unless he has put a ring on it. Let him know that Christ is and always will be your first love. Let him know that for things to go further, he must be a man after God's own heart. Let him know that his eyes must be on Christ, and not on you.

As women, another area we must learn to set standards and boundaries is in our lifestyle habits. When it comes to hygiene, food consumption, the tidiness of your bedroom, etc.; it is so important we adopt respectable and virtuous habits in all of these area's now so we do not struggle when we find ourselves living with our future spouses in our marriages. I will be honest, the tidiness of my bedroom was something I always found to be a challenge, particularly as a female. As females, I'm sure you can agree, we have too many belongings! Too many clothes, too many shoes, too many bags; and so keeping up with managing the orderliness of our bedrooms can be quite a struggle. Especially when you do not even have enough storage space.

However, one thing my mother taught me, after her constant complaints, was even when you do not have enough storage space, there is always a way to keep your room tidy. Get rid of clothes you know you do not wear, shoes you know you do not wear; if you have too many coats and jackets, instead of hanging them inside your wardrobe to take up room, purchase door hangers and hang them behind your door. Make use of storage baskets and place them inside of your wardrobe at the bottom; make use of the space on top of your wardrobe. I had a double bed which basically took up half of my bedroom (my room is a box); so I decided to get a smaller bed to have more space. Laying your bed makes a difference too! My mother always grilled me for not laying my bed. My mother is a clean freak, and so when things are all over the place, it drives her up the wall. However, when I started doing this, I realised laying your bed *actually* makes your room look very tidy and organised; even if other things are all over the place. I've been told that as a female, your bedroom will always portray and describe the kind of person you are. Once you begin to develop and cultivate cleanly and moral habits now, keeping your house tidy and neat in future will not be a struggle. As women, we are the home keepers, therefore if your home is not tidy, it does not give a good impression of you. Develop noble lifestyle habits now, before it is too late.

SET BOUNDARIES, HAVE STANDARDS

Setting godly standards and boundaries will save you from a lot of unnecessary situations, people and lifestyles; simply because you understand that purpose can be aborted if standards and boundaries are not set and respected.

Prayer:

Lord, it is my prayer that You give me the wisdom and direction I need to set the correct, godly standards and boundaries for my life. May You give me the courage and boldness to set these standards and boundaries unapologetically, as well as the ability to adhere to and respect them myself in order for divine purpose to be fulfilled. In Jesus Name, Amen.

"Your life cannot rise any higher than the standards you set or the company you keep."

- Mandy Hale

7

Step Out & Step Up

To walk in the full manifestation of who you are and who God has purposed you to be, you must be willing to step out and step up. Willing to step out of your comfort zone and step up to do the uncomfortable. "Step up & step out" was something God challenged me to do at the beginning of the year 2018. I liked comfortability, I liked being at ease, I was a person who was always content with doing what I knew I could do. I never challenged myself to do more and go beyond. However, 2018 was the year whereby God made me understand I had to bury that mentality and release my full potential in every place I found myself. During that season, I was leading a campus fellowship at my university and was being stretched beyond my capacity in every way, shape and form. As a result, God made it clear to me how I needed to stop holding back and begin releasing everything He had deposited within me regardless of the thoughts, comments, opinions and criticisms of other people.

It is time for all of us to stop holding back from releasing our full potential; we have been comfortable for too long and hiding in our comfort zones for too long. We have been quiet for too long; delaying for too long and idle for too long. It is time to step out and step up because we have ALL been called for such a time as this. Just as Mordecai said to

Esther in Esther 4:14 (NKJV); which was the theme verse God gave to me in order to step out and step up:

> *¹⁴ For if you remain completely silent at this time, relief and deliverance will arise for the Jews from another place, but you and your father's house will perish. Yet who knows whether you have come to the kingdom for such a time as this?"*

A decree had been made whereby all Jews were to be annihilated due to Mordecai's refusal to bow down and pay respect to one of the King's officials; Haman. After hearing this decree, Mordecai wanted to make Esther understand she had not been placed in the palace just for the sake of being in the palace; but that this was the assignment God had given her in order to save and deliver her people. Being the queen in the palace at that time was not a coincidence, it was divine purpose at work. Being the queen gave her the opportunity to influence this decree that was made and turn it around simply because she was the King's babe. When Esther had been informed about the decree that was made, her response to Mordecai made it clear that she did not think she could do anything. She let Mordecai know she would not be able to go to the King unless he had called for her, otherwise there would be a likelihood of her losing her life. I am sure when Mordecai heard this response he thought to himself "is this girl being serious; you are the queen and look at what you are saying". He made it clear to Esther in verse 13 how she should not think she will not die as well just because she is the queen; that if they go down, she'll be going down with them.

Esther had the ability to do something about this situation; this was not the time for her to be sitting on her throne, looking all pretty. She needed to get up and do something! This was her time to step out and step up; it was her responsibility. She could not remain silent; she could not continue sitting down. Mordecai wanted her to recognise she should not wait for somebody else to come and do what God had ordained *her* to do.

Sometimes we become too comfortable with what we do and who we are that we do not see how certain situations are actually *our* responsibility and that *we* have been placed there to bring about change. We always want to wait on the side lines because we think somebody else will come and take the responsibility upon themselves. There is a possibility that it will happen because God is never short of workers, but the sad thing is, it would have been an assignment you would have failed to complete. If you do not rise up, God will raise up another; and when that happens, you have no right to be upset or annoyed because you were given the opportunity.

In the parable of the talents in Matthew 25, the servant who was given 1 talent failed to multiply and increase what he was given and as a result, even the little that was given to him was taken from him and he ended up being thrown into the outer darkness.

The deliverance of the Jews was dependent on Esther. People, nations and generations are depending on you and I to arise, break our silence and walk in purpose. If Esther wasn't going to step up, Mordecai wanted her to know that somebody else would. The healing of certain people is dependent on you. The deliverance of certain people is dependent on you. The manifestation of certain people is dependent on you. You have a responsibility; don't allow somebody to take that responsibility from your hands.

Esther found herself in an unfamiliar setting and situation; she had been chosen by God to be queen amongst the many other women that could have also been chosen. It is possible that when she was chosen, she thought to herself "why me?". Sometimes God will position you in places and situations whereby you will not understand how you got there and why you are even there. In those situations, that is when you simply begin to trust God and remember that the God whom you serve is truly purposeful. When you have been placed in an unfamiliar situation, know that God is already familiar with it; and if God is already familiar with it, you have nothing to worry about. Do not fight against it and run away from unfamiliar situations because when you do, you are ultimately running away from developing and growing in purpose.

The first time I was asked to lead an opening prayer for a youth programme we were holding at my church was the worst experience of my life. My voice was shaking, my legs were shaking, I was wearing heeled shoes as well so that didn't help; I was sweating, it was just an awful experience. Afterwards, I told my youth president not to ask me to do anything like that again because I would not do it. It was an uncomfortable situation even though I "stepped out". However, what I failed to realise is that it was an opportunity for me to be uncomfortable in order for me to be comfortable. That was the first time I had ever held a mic in front of people and spoke, but it was not the last. From that experience, God was preparing me for what was yet to come. God does not place you in uncomfortable situations to disgrace you but to develop you and grow you. Esther's act of remaining in an unfamiliar situation resulted in the lives of many people being saved. Embrace the uncomfortable!

~ Salt and Light ~

In Matthew 5:13-16, Jesus teaches us that we are the salt of the earth. We know salt is an ingredient that gives flavour to food and is sometimes what could either make or destroy the food. Being the salt of the earth, we are supposed to bring flavour to this earth; we are the ones to make a difference to the way the earth tastes. Our lives must have substance; the same way salt gives substance to food, that is the same way our lives must have that extra and transformational ingredient that will bring change to the earth we live in.

Salt also preserves; to preserve means to protect, defend and care for. We have the responsibility of protecting the earth and not harming it. There was a dream God gave me whereby I was hoovering the street outside of my house. There was so much litter on the floor, so I was given a hoover to start hoovering the concrete ground (weird, I know). What He made me understand was I have a responsibility of cleaning the mess that has already been made on this earth. We hear of global warming and how it just seems to be getting worse and worse; we are the ones to be at fault for that. We are failing to protect and care for the earth we are living in; we litter instead of simply putting our rubbish in public bins; we urinate outside instead of waiting to get to our homes or finding a decent place to urinate; we spit on the ground instead of finding some tissue to spit on. Let us not only be salt in the four walls of the church building and on our church compound but everywhere else we find ourselves.

We were given the instruction by God in Genesis 1 to manage and subdue the earth, and everything that is in it. To look after the earth *is* our responsibility.

We cannot be salt that has lost its flavour; if salt has lost its flavour, it would be as though it is not even present in the first place simply because the existence of salt without flavour is useless, worthless and valueless. As a Purpose Driven Woman, do not let your existence become non-existent simply because you lack flavour, influence and substance. Your existence is meant to bring out the best flavour of the earth. The truth of the matter is when you do not have flavour, influence or substance, people will disregard you, people will walk over you and will not acknowledge your value. People will not give you their ear or attention if you do not have anything good or meaningful to offer. As a Purpose Driven Woman, your existence needs to be recognised and valued simply because of what you have and possess. You should be the person people will come to for solutions, counsel and answers.

In this world full of sin, darkness and evil, you are the light this world needs. When the bible makes reference to the word *'world'* in this passage of scripture, it refers to the governing systems, political systems, constitutions and world affairs. Therefore, you are the light that needs to shine in the government, in politics, in education, in the economy, in entertainment, in the health sector. All of these places have been polluted and blinded by the ways of the devil. Gross darkness has filled all of these spheres, but we must purpose in our hearts to bring light to these places. A place without light will make it hard for you to navigate around it, but when light is made available, you become exposed to what is around you and everything becomes clear. Even though everything was already there, because there was no light and you did not know, you were lost and ignorant.

We must become the available light to all people so that whenever they are around us, light is given to their situations, solutions are given to their problems, clarity is given to their concerns, and everything which was hidden from them will be exposed simply because of our light. There are certain people who have been placed in positions of influence, but are blind, lost and confused! They do not know what decisions they need to take and what actions they need to implement; they need your light! People should see that there is something different about you when they are around you. Everything about your light should radiate God. God is not to be hidden; He *is* what the world needs.

A city that has been placed on a hill cannot be hidden; whatever you do to try and hide it, it will not work. It has been placed above all things and is visible to everything. A city placed on a hilltop will be seen by everyone by force, simply because of where it has been placed. It is positioned in such a way that even if it is not asked to be seen, it will be seen. That is the kind of presence we must carry as a child and daughter of God. The presence of God in our lives must be so contagious and tangible when people encounter us or even just walk past us. Regardless of whatever we may try to do to hide it, it cannot be hidden.

The fact Jesus said we are "a city on a hill" and not a town or a village is very significant. A city has more value placed on it than a town or village. People are able to remember and recall names of cities more than towns and villages. A city has greater attractions than a town or a village; it is much bigger in size and population and has more recognition. What is Jesus trying to say here? You being a city, you must portray yourself as such. You must understand you are valuable and that much value has been placed upon you. And because much value has been placed upon you, what you are able to give out also carries value. You possess influential characteristics and qualities. You are not just anybody, what you have and carry has the ability to affect cities, countries and nations!

Matthew 5:15 NKJV:

> *¹⁵ No one lights a lamp and then puts it under a basket. Instead, a lamp is placed on a stand, where it gives light to everyone in the house.*

What is the use of a lamp being on but hidden? It is useless. Many of us can be likened to a lamp that is on but hidden. We know we carry something great, we know we have such great potential, we know what we can bring to the table, but then we hide ourselves and portray ourselves in a way that we do not know any better. This was so me! I would always find myself in situations whereby I would have so much to say concerning topics and matters being discussed in the midst of people, but because of fear and lack of confidence in myself and what I possess, I would never speak. God did not place His light, gifts, potential, abilities within you for you to hide them. He placed them within you for you to make use of them and make impact. Do not hide yourself under a basket; you were made to shine bright, your purpose was made to shine bright, everything within you was made to shine bright! Do not dim the brightness of your lamp in order to make yourself and others feel more comfortable. Do not lose your usefulness and value by hiding your 'lamp' under a basket.

The purpose of a lamp is to shine and give light; therefore, it must be placed on a lampstand where its *purpose* to give out light can be fulfilled. Nobody will be able to see what you have and possess unless you show them and make it known. The same way a lamp must be placed on a stand in order for it to function according to its purpose is the same way you must position yourself in a way whereby you can show what you have and function according to your purpose. You must come to a place whereby you are no longer comfortable with just *knowing* that you have a gift and carry something great, but that you become intentional about how that gift is shared and used to influence your surroundings. It is not every day you must wait to be called on to do something by people, sometimes you must take the initiative, step out in faith and do what you *already* know God has called you to do. Sometimes, we're so comfortable and content with knowing what God has said concerning our lives; we get excited when we hear prophecies about our destiny and purpose, but are not willing to do something about the prophecy. We get so caught up in what God has said that we forget we actually need to step out and *do* what He has said. We forget that we have a part to play in bringing that prophecy to manifestation. There are certain prophecies which do take time to manifest, but there are some that require you to make a move. Some of us have missed out on the fulfilment of a prophecy for our lives not because the prophecy wasn't true or genuine, but because we failed to act upon it. We must get to a place whereby we are **not** just comfortable with receiving prophetic words and doing nothing about it.

On the other hand, it is also important that you do this will all **humility**. God does not desire you to showcase what you possess for you to feel good about yourself or to behave as though you are the only one who has been called or has a gift, no. He desires you to showcase what you have in order for Him to receive glory and acknowledgement, for others to be encouraged to also showcase what they have. This part of the scripture can be easily misinterpreted and wrongly applied as some may see it as an opportunity to go and draw attention to themselves through their gifting's and abilities, forgetting they are to bring attention and glory to God through it. It takes humility to function effectively in your purpose. Your number one motive for *not* hiding your lamp under a basket and placing it on a stand for all to see should be to glorify God; that men may give glory to Him, not to attract opportunities. Once you focus on glorifying God, He will take care of the opportunities. He will cause your gifting's to open doors for you and bring you before great people (Proverbs 18:16).

Also, you should not think hiding your lamp under a basket is humility; that's false humility. Knowing you possess something that will bring change and transform your world, and hiding it is you basically robbing God of glory that is meant to be given to Him. Real humility is to use your gift to acknowledge the Giver of your gift.

Wherever you are placed, you are there to fulfil purpose. A lamp can be placed anywhere; on a chair, on a table, on the floor; the most important thing is that it is fulfilling purpose wherever it *has* been placed.

~ The Daughters of Zelophehad ~

The story of the daughters of Zelophehad is found in the book of Numbers chapter 27. These women were bold, fearless and courageous; they stepped out! They were women who knew who they were and exercised the authority and potential they possessed. At the time, a law had been put in place whereby all families who did not have any sons or males at all would not receive an inheritance or any property in the land the Israelites were promised.

These women had no brothers, and their father had died in the wilderness. However, regardless of the law that had been put in place concerning inheritance, these women stepped out in faith and demanded what belonged to them and their family. They knew what had happened to them was not fair and so did something about it. They didn't sit down, cry and complain, but they stood together as sisters and went to make their request. They went to stand not only in front of Moses, but before Eleazer the priest, the tribal leaders and the entire community. You could imagine the pressure; however, that did not stop them. Five ladies against these high positioned people making a request that could have potentially been dismissed as soon as they opened their mouths. This teaches us how we should never be fearful or afraid of stepping out of our comfort zones to do what we know we need to do in order to achieve something.

When making their 'request', these women did not ask, they demanded. They said in verse 4 *"give us"*, it was a demand and a command. It was faith-filled speech; the kind of speech that believes it will receive what is being demanded. The kind of speech that has no ounce of doubt in it. Sometimes, it is not only in the things we do that we must step out and step up, but also in the things we say. A Purpose Driven Woman is a woman who speaks with authority and boldness.

Powerfully, we see their faith-filled speech brought them faith-filled results. The Lord granted them their demand and instructed Moses to give them their inheritance. Not only that, the bold and fearless act of these sisters caused God to even change His mind concerning the existing law regarding the inheritance. Their act of faith brought a significant change in history for families who had no sons. They left a legacy. What these sisters did, did not only benefit them but other families. Your act of faith could be the very thing that will bring a change to the state of the government, the church, the education system, the state of the entertainment sector and so on. Don't let your unwillingness to act hinder your generation and the world from receiving and benefitting. Every act of faith is accompanied by a great and unexpected result from God. What great result have you been delaying because of your unwillingness to step out in faith? That step of faith is the very thing that will bring the result and the change you keep praying for.

The name "Zelophehad" means 'protection from fear'. These daughters literally lived and walked by the meaning of their father's name. These daughters represented the name of their father even when he was dead; simply because of their act of boldness. The bible is very purposeful for mentioning the name of their father; it didn't need to because all 5 of their names had been mentioned anyway. However, it is what these 5 sisters did that caused them to be *identified* as Zelophehad's daughters. How much more we that our Father is the God in Heaven; who is the Most High God, the Covenant Keeping God, our Protector, our Counsellor, our Strength, our Grace, our Shepherd, our Abba! We carry His name simply because we are His daughters; therefore, we must live by the name of our Father. We must ask ourselves whether what we do; our acts of faith, courage, boldness and fearlessness, cause us to be identified as "daughters of El-Shaddai". Everything we do must be able to represent our Father in every way. Step out of your comfort zone in faith and let your boldness cause you to be identified as a daughter of Yahweh.

    We must be willing to release all that is on the inside of us because it is actually possible to be out of your comfort zone but yet still in it. You are fully and completely out of your comfort zone when you are able to release your FULL potential; not 50%, not 83%, not 99%, but 100%. Yes, you may have stepped out to do something you have never done before and released the 10% of potential, but why is the remaining 90% being held back? Sometimes you may only release the 10% because that is what you feel comfortable releasing. Do you see how we are back to comfortability? You are out of your comfort zone by releasing the 10%, but still in it by holding back the 90%. Release the remaining 90%; release the full potential; don't hold anything back. Release, release, release. Step out and step up!

STEP OUT & STEP UP

Prayer:

Lord, thank You for making me come to the understanding that I cannot sit on my gifting's and my potential any longer. Thank you for making me understand that releasing what I possess is for Your glory alone. I rebuke every spirit of comfortability, fear and doubt that may be causing me to remain silent and lack confidence. I pray for the boldness, fearlessness and courage to step out and step up. Make me as bold as a lioness, in Jesus Name I Pray, Amen.

"We need to be taken out of our comfort zone to the extent that it becomes comfortable."

- *Henry Agyeman*

8

The Time Is NOW

PURPOSE DRIVEN WOMAN

Isaiah 60:1-3 NKJV

> *Arise, shine;*
> *For your light has come!*
> *And the glory of the* LORD *is risen upon you.*
> *² For behold, the darkness shall cover the earth,*
> *And deep darkness the people;*
> *But the* LORD *will arise over you,*
> *And His glory will be seen upon you.*
> *³ The Gentiles shall come to your light,*
> *And kings to the brightness of your rising.*

The time has come for you to arise and shine! The time is indeed now to walk and operate in the FULL manifestation of who you are and who God has destined you to be. The time is indeed now for you to live and walk as a Purpose Driven Woman. In every environment you find yourself, in whichever season you are currently in, you can and must fulfil purpose. The world and the earth is in need of your influence, in need of your abilities, in need of your qualities; so let us arise as women of purpose and be intentional about how we can share these things with the world. You alone know what you possess and you alone know what you can share, all I can do is encourage and motivate you to come to this realisation and share it. The scripture says darkness shall cover this earth and deep darkness the people; it is a prophetic message which we are seeing come to fulfilment now. The scripture makes it clear that the darkness which covers the people is deeper and more severe than the darkness that covers the earth; the deeper darkness that has overcome the people is what will result in the blindness of the people to intensify and escalate. The earth will encounter chaos and the people will fail to recognise the right solution for the chaos: Jesus Christ. Nevertheless, we are also made to understand that the Lord will arise over us. He is not arising over us to protect us from the darkness, but to bring the light we possess to eliminate the darkness. Gentiles coming to your light and kings to the brightness of your rising symbolises relevance, influence and impact! As a result of the influence you are having in your world, important, relevant and influential people will be attracted to you, whereby they come to know the God you serve! Only if you arise and shine!

Matthew 22:14 NKJV:

"Many are called but few are chosen."

You have a specific call of God upon your life, but it is up to you as to whether you want to be chosen by choosing to walk in that calling. God is not looking for those who are only *aware* of His calling but those who are also *obedient* to the calling. Jonah was aware, but he wasn't obedient, the first time. Jonah was aware but he didn't fulfil the command. You may be aware of the call of God upon your life today, but be reminded that to be aware isn't enough, it is the first step but you must purpose in your heart to be obedient: The Time Is Now. God is seeking your obedience now.

Before I started writing this book, I was seeking confirmation after confirmation. I was being so stubborn. I would be watching sermons, reading social media posts, having conversations with people, and all the things I would be hearing was confirming that God was telling me to write this book. The day after I received the instruction, God began revealing unto me all the titles for the chapters that would be in the book. Yet, I was still being stubborn, and *still* wanted more confirmation. The excuses were many; until I truly just had to slap myself and remind myself of what God had said to me: The Time Is Now! I had to be obedient.

Another reason for being quite reluctant and hesitant in actually following through with this assignment was because the topic of "Purpose" being spoken about everywhere. Sermons, YouTube videos, Instagram pages, Facebook posts; the topic was really trending. As a result, I began thinking to myself and asking myself, "what more am

THE TIME IS NOW

I actually going to bring? I will just be adding to what is already out there, so what is the point.". Really and truly, it was just the enemy trying to plant lies in my mind. When God gives you an instruction to carry out an assignment, the devil will always *try* and make you feel unqualified or mediocre. He will by all means try to make you feel as though what you have to offer is not worth sharing just because it may already be out there. The devil is a liar.

We must remember when God has called us to do something, He is the One who will make room for us and He is the One who will cause us to be relevant, regardless of how saturated the sphere or field is. My purpose is unique and your purpose is unique, even if it is similar. Your purpose will always have an unprecedented and distinct element to it; therefore, when you are pursuing it, pursue it **unapologetically** and with all that you have! Making reference to John the Baptist once again; he knew his purpose was similar to Jesus Christ's, but yet, he still operated effectively in it.

John 9:4-5 NKJV:

> *⁴ I must work the works of Him who sent Me while it is day; the night is coming when no one can work. ⁵ As long as I am in the world, I am the light of the world."*

Jesus Christ, our ultimate example, was given authority over the earth in order to save mankind, and when He came, He did just that. Jesus was basically saying in the verse above that whilst He is alive, He must complete all the work He was sent to do; ALL. There was basically no time to waste. He made it clear that He is the light of the world *as long* as He is still in it, so until He goes, it is still day. In other words, it is still time to do the work if He is in the world.

As we have learnt previously, we are the light of the world, so we must ensure we are doing all that we *know* we need to do to complete the works we were sent to do before the night comes, before we leave. Jesus knew His days had been numbered and so had to fulfil every assignment over His life whilst He had the time and opportunity to do so. He took advantage of every opportunity to manifest the power and glory of His ministry.

The bible makes us to understand that we should ask God to teach us to number our days so we may gain a heart of wisdom (Psalm 90:12). In other words; we must not think we have all the time in the world, we must not have it in our minds that we will only begin to live out the purpose God has for us when we reach a certain age or stage in our lives. We must take advantage of every day so that we will gain wisdom on how to live and *how* to take advantage of every day. In due course, because we know our days are numbered, we will seek the wisdom of God and the counsel of God in order to know *what* we need to do and *how* we must do it. Jesus made sure He gave His best when He came on earth, and He certainly did. He gave His life! That is why when all had ended, He was able to say "it is finished". He fulfilled every assignment that had been assigned to His life by His Father. It is time for us to purpose in our hearts to do the same as Purpose Driven Women.

The Time Is Now.

Prayer:

Father, grace me, help me, strengthen me, EMPOWER me and ENABLE me to live, walk and operate in the FULL manifestation of who I AM. Who I ALREADY AM from the inside, from the womb, from the belly. Father, let it begin to manifest now! Teach me Lord to also number my days so that I may gain a heart of wisdom to fulfil purpose. In Jesus Name I Pray, Amen.

"God is aware of everything He has deposited in you; so have confidence in the confidence that He has in you."

- Daniella Akosua

THE TIME IS NOW

Who is a Purpose Driven Woman?

A woman who is driven by purpose; whereby everything she does in life and everything she pursues in life is driven by her desire and determination to fulfil purpose. She is a woman who understands that there is a certain life she must live in order to be purpose driven and fulfil purpose. She is a woman who WALKS with God, and as a result is a woman who is LED by the Spirit of God in everything. She understands she has been born on purpose for a purpose for such a time as this and so does ALL that she knows she needs to do in order to accomplish God's preordained assignment/s for her life. She is a woman on a mission to walk and live in the FULL manifestation of who God created her to be before the beginning of time.

She is you.

Author Bio

Daniella A. Appiah Agyeman is a young woman who, like many other young women, desires to be a woman after God's own heart. She rededicated her life to Christ at the age of 16 and has purposed in her heart to never look back since; though the journey has not been an easy and smooth one. She is currently a youth leader at her church, and a female mentor to a few younger women. She strongly believes that Purpose Driven Woman is more than a book, but a ministry and a movement that God has birthed on the inside of her to execute and establish.

Daniella has three brothers and is the only daughter among the siblings. She lives in the UK, but desires to reach nations with the message/s God continues to lay on her heart.

You can stay connected with Daniella via Instagram: @daniellaakosua_ and Facebook: Daniella Akosua Appiah.

Made in the USA
Middletown, DE
29 June 2023